A Basic Guide to Understanding Guardianship, Conservatorship, Powers of Attorney, Medical Advance Directives, and Representative Payeeship: Developed for Use by County Adult Protective Services Caseworkers and Supervisors

Colorado Division of Aging and Adult Services

A Basic Guide to Understanding

Guardianship, Conservatorship, Powers of Attorney, Medical Advance Directives, and Representative Payeeship

Developed For Use by County Adult Protective Services
Caseworkers and Supervisors

October 2003

cdhs
Colorado Department of Human Services
people who help people

Introduction and Overview

This manual was written to assist Colorado Adult Protective Services (APS) caseworkers in carrying out various forms of legal authority, and to direct clients and others. The manual may be helpful to other professionals who work closely with at-risk adults such as ombudsmen, law enforcement personnel, professional caregivers, advocates for elderly persons or for persons with disabilities, health care personnel, and staff of agencies and organizations who work with clients that have needs related to various forms of authority.

Forms of legal authority addressed in this manual include guardianship, conservatorship, powers of attorney, advance directives, and representative payeeship. Each topic is divided into separate sections that include definitions, procedures, professional responsibilities, and relevant statutes. Separate sections on abuse of authority and resources are additionally included.

A primary goal in writing this manual is to provide information that outlines complex processes and statutes in easy to understand terminology. It is written to guide county staff who are unfamiliar with the process of filing petitions or assuming guardianship responsibility; to serve as a training tool for counties that have staff who require an orientation to legal forms of authority; and for APS staff and other professionals who need a refresher or reference guide to answer general questions about various forms of legal authority. This manual is not intended as a stand alone or comprehensive legal guide for obtaining or understanding forms of authority. The contents of this manual should be supplemented with reference to statutes and with consultation from county attorneys and other legal representatives.

This manual represents the synthesis of numerous handbooks, articles, presentations, and other manuals from a variety of sources. Some of the content was summarized or extrapolated from materials that were developed by Alice Kitt, Director of Guardianship Alliance of Colorado, Attorney Carl Glatstein, elder law attorney and partner in the law firm Glatstein and O'Brien, LLP, and Attorney Susan Fox Buchanan, elder law attorney specializing in end of life issues and medical ethics with the law firm Buchanan & Stouffer, P.C. Additionally, information regarding representative payeeships was obtained from published information prepared by the Social Security Administration.

The Colorado State Adult Protective Services program wishes to graciously acknowledge Alice Kitt, Attorney Carl Glatstein, and Attorney Susan Fox Buchanan for their reviews and helpful suggestions regarding the manual. Special recognition goes to State APS program specialists Pat Stanis and Peg Rogers for their expertise and commitment in constructing this educational resource for the dedicated professionals who provide protective and supportive services to at-risk adults in Colorado.

Paulette St James

Paulette St James LCSW, PhD
APS Program Administrator
Division of Aging and Adult Services
Office of Adult, Disability, and Rehabilitation Services
Colorado Department of Human Services

Dedication

The Colorado Adult Protective Services program dedicates this manual to Alice Kitt and Carl Glatstein for their exceptional contributions to promote the rights of at-risk adults in Colorado by providing services and education in the areas of guardianship and other levels of authority for at-risk adults.

Alice Kitt is the founder and president of The Guardianship Alliance of Colorado and has played a major role in the promotion, recruitment, and oversight of volunteer guardians in Denver, and surrounding areas. She provides individual counseling and assistance, guardianship training, public speaking, program development, and service delivery systems advocacy. Alice has devoted many hours traveling around the state to educate communities and promote the development of community groups that will accept and oversee guardianship arrangements. Prior to her current endeavors, Alice was instrumental in the development, promotion, and implementation of federal legislation specific to American citizens with developmental disabilities. Alice's devotion and commitment to the rights of the at-risk adult are exemplary.

Carl Glatstein has practiced law in Colorado for 19 years. He is a partner in the Denver law firm, Glatstein & O'Brien, LLP. For the past thirteen years, he has worked primarily in the field of Elder Law. He proved to be an excellent leader as co-chair for the Colorado Bar Association (CBA) Joint Subcommittee on the Uniform Guardianship and Protective Proceedings Act (1997-2000), enacted in 2000. In this role, Carl worked with many community entities, including county human service agencies, in developing and revising forms and procedures that pertain to guardianship arrangements. Carl serves as a member of the CBA Elder Law Forum Committee and Trust & Estate Section, the Denver Community Bioethics Committee, the University of Denver Elder Law Institute, the Adams County community Adult Protection team, the Guardianship Alliance of Colorado, and the National Academy of Elder Law Attorneys.

Alice and Carl continue to make outstanding contributions to the health, safety, and welfare of some of Colorado's most vulnerable adults. Colorado Adult Protective Services programs are very fortunate to have two outstanding professionals working for the protection of at-risk adults.

Guardianship

This section of the manual defines terms used in guardianship proceedings, describes the procedures involved in obtaining a guardianship, describes the duties of a guardian, and provides information on changing guardians when necessary. Responding to allegations of abuse of guardianship authority and other types of authority positions is addressed later in this manual.

The following terms regarding guardianship are used in this manual:

> - **"Adult"** refers to the person 18 years of age or older for whom the guardianship is being considered before a petition for guardianship is filed with the court.
> - **"Respondent"** refers to the person for whom the guardianship is being considered once a petition for guardianship has been filed with the court.
> - **"Ward"** refers to the person for whom the guardianship was granted by the court.
> - **"Incapacitated"** refers to an inability to effectively receive and/or evaluate information or an inability to make and/or communicate decisions to such an extent that physical health or safety is in jeopardy.
> - **"Guardian ad litem"** (GAL) is a person appointed by the court to take legal action on behalf of the respondent. The guardian ad litem is charged with representing and making recommendations that are in the respondent's best interest. (For more detailed information on GAL, read the Colorado Revised Statutes (C.R.S.) 15-10-403 (5), C.R.S. 15-14-115 and Rule 15, Colorado Rules of Probate Procedure.)

A **guardianship** is a court appointment that gives a person or an organization responsibility and authority for making decisions on behalf of an individual who is unable to manage his/her own affairs and make his/her own decisions. Guardianship for adults in Colorado is authorized by C.R.S. Title 15, Article 14, Part 3. This statute is included at the end of this section. Instructions for accessing statutes on the Internet are located in the Resource section of this manual.

Types of Guardianship

There are three basic types of guardianship available through the Colorado courts. They are:

- Emergency (formerly temporary)
- Limited
- Unlimited

The court may appoint an **emergency** guardian when substantial harm to the respondent's health, safety, or welfare is likely to occur without intervention. Emergency guardianship is limited to 60 days. Appointment of an attorney for the respondent is mandatory and continues throughout the emergency guardianship. Appointment of an emergency guardian is not a determination of incapacity.

The appointment of a **limited** guardianship grants only those powers to the guardian needed by the ward due to the ward's limitations. Limitations are included in the court order of appointment.

An **unlimited** guardianship grants all decision-making powers to the guardian. The court will require sufficient justification as to why a limited guardianship should not be granted.

In all cases, the court will make every effort to encourage the development of the ward's maximum self-reliance and independence.

Procedure for Obtaining a Guardianship of Any Type

There are several procedures to follow in obtaining a guardianship. The following information outlines the typical processes involved in obtaining a guardianship appointment. It is advisable to consult with the local county attorney regarding specific legal issues.

Preliminary Procedures and Information

1) A **petition** for "Appointment of a Guardian for an Incapacitated Person" must be filed with the district court in the county where the alleged incapacitated client lives. One exception is in Denver County where the petition is filed with the probate court. A petition can be filed by any interested party.

2) A **filing fee** is required when the petition is filed. If appropriate, the court may waive the fee based on the respondent or petitioner's inability to pay.

3) **Medical information** in the form of a functional evaluation should be submitted with the petition to describe the client's lack of decision-making capacity. Filing without medical information is possible in exceptional circumstances.

   a. The medical information can be a letter or report from a physician, a psychologist, or another individual qualified to evaluate the respondent's alleged incapacity.
   b. The evaluation report must contain all of the following:
      - A description of the nature, type, and extent of the respondent's specific cognitive and functional limitations, if any.
      - An evaluation of the respondent's mental and physical condition and, if appropriate, educational potential, adaptive behavior, and social skills.
      - A prognosis for improvement and a recommendation as to the appropriate treatment or rehabilitation plan.
      - The date of any assessment or examination upon which the report is based.
   c. If an evaluation is not submitted with the petition, the court *may* order an evaluation. If the respondent requests an evaluation, the court *must* order an evaluation.

4) A **statement of the type of guardianship** requested must be filed with the petition. The court presumes that a limited guardianship is necessary in order to preserve the rights of the respondent to manage as many of his/her own affairs as possible while still providing necessary protection and oversight. The petition must include:

   a. The type of guardianship requested (emergency, limited, unlimited).

b. The extent of decision making authority requested.
c. If a limited guardianship is requested, it may include the authority to make:
- Only medical decisions
- Only placement decisions
- Only financial decisions
- A combination of medical, placement or financial decisions
d. A petition for an unlimited guardianship must state the reason why an unlimited guardianship is necessary.

5) A general **statement of the respondent's property** must be filed. This statement must include:

a. An estimate of the property's value
b. The value of the adult's life insurance
c. The value of the adult's pension and/or other financial assets
d. The source and amount of any other anticipated income

6) The order of **priorities for appointment** as guardian are:

a. Current court-appointed guardian
b. Respondent's nominee
c. Agent under health care power of attorney
d. Agent under general power of attorney
e. Spouse or spouse's nominee in will or other writing
f. Adult child of the respondent
g. Parent or parent's nominee
h. Adult with whom respondent resided for 6 out of 12 months preceding the filing of the petition

7) **The court may prohibit some persons or service providers from guardianship** appointments due to concerns regarding dual role conflicts. The court may make an exception for good cause. Examples of persons who may be excluded from consideration of a guardianship appointment due to a dual role conflict are:

a. Long-term care providers unless related by blood or marriage
b. Paid professionals who are serving the same ward as both:
- A guardian and a conservator
- A guardian and a direct service provider
- A conservator and a direct service provider

8) Once a petition has been filed, a **notice** must be *personally* served to the respondent. (It is not necessary to hire a process server.)

a. The "Notice of a Hearing on the Petition" must be served:
- At least 10 days before the hearing

- By any person who does not have an interest in the outcome of the guardianship proceedings.
    b. The notice must include:
      - A copy of the petition
      - Information regarding the respondent's required presence at the hearing, unless excused by the court
      - Information about the respondent's rights at the hearing
      - The nature, purpose, and consequences of the guardianship appointment

9) A **notice of the guardianship hearing** must be served to all persons listed on the petition as **interested persons**. Interested persons may include, but are not limited to:

   a. Respondent's spouse
   b. Respondent's adult children and parents (if none, then next closest relative)
   c. Each person responsible for the care or custody of the respondent
   d. Respondent's treating physician
   e. Each legal representative of the respondent
   f. Each person nominated as a guardian by the respondent

10) A **court visitor** is assigned by the court to act as an investigator for the court. The investigation process for the court visitor includes the following:

   a. A meeting with the respondent in order to explain:
      - The substance of the petition
      - The nature, purpose, and effect of the proceeding
      - The general powers and duties of a guardian
      - The rights of the respondent
      - Costs and expenses of the proceeding
   b. An interview of the petitioner and the proposed guardian (if different from the petitioner).
   c. A visit to the present and proposed dwellings of the respondent.
   d. Information obtained from any physician or other person who is known to have treated, advised, or assessed the respondent's relevant physical or mental condition.
   e. Any other investigation that the court directs.
   f. A report to the court on the visitor's findings that should include the following:
      - A recommendation as to whether an attorney and/or a guardian ad litem should be appointed.
      - A summary of daily functions the respondent can manage without assistance; those he/she could manage with the assistance of supportive services or benefits, including use of appropriate technological assistance; and those he/she cannot manage.
      - Recommendations regarding the appropriateness of guardianship.
      - Whether less restrictive means of intervention are available.
      - The type of guardianship and, if limited, the powers to be granted.

- The qualifications of the guardian.
- Whether the respondent approves or disapproves of the proposed guardian, the powers and duties proposed, and the scope of the guardianship.
- Whether the proposed dwelling meets the respondent's individual needs.
- A recommendation of whether a professional evaluation or further evaluation is necessary.
- Any other matters that the court directs.

Hearing Procedures and Information

11) The guardianship statute specifies the **respondent's rights** at the hearing. The respondent has the right to:

a. Have notice of, and be present at, any court proceeding concerning issues related to his/her guardianship appointment.
b. See or hear all the evidence bearing on his/her condition.
c. Be represented by counsel of choice or court-appointed counsel.
d. Present evidence.
e. Cross-examine witnesses, including any court-appointed visitor, evaluator, or physician.
f. Contest the petition.
g. Object to the appointment of the proposed guardian or his/her powers or duties.
h. Object to the creation of the proposed guardianship, its scope, or duration.
i. Have a guardian ad litem appointed to represent his/her best interests, if the court determines that a need for such representation exists.
j. Know that all costs and expenses of the proceeding, including attorney fees, will be paid from his/her estate, unless otherwise directed by the court.

12) The guardianship statute clarifies **who is required to attend** the hearing.

a. The petitioner must make reasonable efforts to secure the respondent's attendance at the hearing.
   - The respondent must attend the hearing unless excused by the court for good cause.
   - The court may hold the hearing in a manner that reasonably accommodates the respondent, such as by telephone or in the respondent's place of residence.
b. The petitioner and proposed guardian (if different) must attend the hearing. The court may allow these parties to appear by telephone in exceptional circumstances.
c. The hearing is open to the public.
   - The respondent or any other interested person showing good cause may request the hearing be closed.

- If the respondent objects to a request for a closed hearing, it must remain open.
  d. Any person who has obtained the court's permission may participate in the proceeding.

13) A **decision by the court to grant guardianship** can only be made if the court finds by clear and convincing evidence that the respondent is an incapacitated person. Based on the degree of incapacity, the court will limit the guardian's powers to encourage maximum self-reliance and independence of the ward.

Following the Hearing

14) Within 30 days, the guardian must **send a notice of the guardianship appointment** to the ward and those interested parties who were given notice of the original petition. The notice must include a copy of:

a. Notice of appointment and right to request termination or modification
b. Court order

15) The **reports required** by the court from the guardian include:

a. An initial guardian report that must be filed within 60 days after appointment
b. An annual guardian report that must be filed on the anniversary of the appointment

16) The guardian must send **copies of the initial and annual reports to the ward** and interested persons, along with a notice of filing the reports.

17) The guardian must provide **post-appointment hearing notices** to the ward and any others that the court requires.

Duties and Powers of a Guardian

Duties of a Guardian

A guardian is expected to understand and carry out the responsibilities outlined in the specific guardianship orders. When in doubt about the authority to decide on a specific matter, a guardian should seek prior approval from the court. While individual guardianship orders may contain specific instructions, there are general duties and responsibilities that every guardian is expected to fulfill. Colorado statute gives guardians authority to make the following decisions regarding the ward's support, care, education, health, and welfare.

A guardian must:

1) **Become or remain personally acquainted** with the ward and maintain sufficient contact to know of the ward's capacities, limitations, needs, opportunities, and physical and mental health.

2) Make arrangements for, keep informed about, and **maintain documentation** of the ward's current situation regarding:

   a. Finances
   b. Living arrangements and care givers
   c. Health and medical care
   d. Education and training, personal needs
   e. Preferences and desires
   f. Employment, recreation, and leisure time

3) **Become acquainted with the people who are significant in the ward's life** such as family, doctors, nurses, recreation directors, case workers, employers, therapists, teachers, friends, and neighbors.

4) **Take reasonable care of the ward's personal effects** and bring protective proceedings, if necessary, to protect the property of the ward.

5) **Appropriately spend the ward's money, that is in the guardian's control**, for the ward's current support, care, education, health, and welfare needs.

6) **Save any of the ward's excess money** for the ward's future needs. If a conservator is appointed for the ward, the guardian must pay the excess money to the conservator, at least quarterly, to be saved for the ward's future needs.

   a. If the ward has substantial assets (more than the amount required for his/her daily living needs), it is necessary that a conservator be appointed.

b. The process for appointment of a conservator (refer to the Conservatorship section of this manual) is similar to that for a guardian. If the ward is a relative of the guardian, it may be possible for the guardian to serve as both guardian and conservator.

7) **Inform the court of any change** in the ward's residence.

8) **Immediately notify the court if the ward's condition has changed** to the degree that guardianship may no longer be necessary.

9) **Immediately notify the court of the ward's death.**

Powers of a Guardian

Unless limited by the court order, guardians have the power to:

1) **Consent to medical or other care, treatment, or service for the ward**. Guardians must respect the ward's wishes and directions contained in any current advance directives.

2) **Apply for and receive money payable to the ward**, guardian, or custodian for the support of the ward from any government or private source.

3) **Take custody of the ward** and decide where the ward is to live. *Out of state moves require specific permission from the court.*

4) **Take necessary actions to force an obligated party to support the ward** or to pay money for the benefit of the ward if there is no conservator.

5) **Petition the court for authority to consent to the adoption or marriage** of the ward.

6) **Petition the court for authority to apply for a divorce or legal separation** on behalf of the ward if it is in the best interest of the ward.

Rights, Immunities and Limitations of a Guardian

1) With approval by the court, guardians may receive **reasonable compensation** for services as a guardian and reimbursement for room and board provided by the guardian or one affiliated with the guardian. If there is a conservator, other than the guardian or one affiliated with the guardian, reasonable compensation and reimbursement to the guardian may be paid by the conservator without a court order.

2) Guardians are **not required to provide for their ward**, or pay for their ward's expenses, **out of the guardian's own funds**. However, if a guardian signs an agreement or contract personally accepting financial liability, the guardian may be held personally liable.

3) Guardians are **not liable to third parties for acts of the ward** solely because of the guardianship.

4) Guardians who exercise reasonable care in selecting parties to provide medical or other care, treatment, or service for the ward, are **not liable for injury to the ward resulting from the negligent or wrongful conduct of the providers**.

5) **Guardians may not consent to involuntary commitment, or care and treatment** of a ward for mental illness, developmental disabilities, or for alcoholism or substance abuse. In all of these instances, a guardian must proceed under the appropriate statute.

Reports To the Court

Within 60 days of appointment, or as otherwise directed by the court, guardians must submit a written report to the court. This report should be on the Colorado probate code form titled "Initial Guardian's Report." Instructions on how to access this and other guardianship forms on the Internet is located in the Resource section of this manual.

1) The initial report must include:

   a. The condition of the ward.
   b. The guardian's personal care plan for the ward.
   c. An accounting of money and other assets in the guardian's possession or control.

2) On each anniversary of the guardian appointment, guardians must submit an annual "Guardian Report" to the court that includes:

   a. The current mental, physical, and social condition of the ward.
   b. The ward's living arrangements.
   c. Medical, educational, and vocational services provided and the adequacy of the ward's care.
   d. A summary of the guardian's visits with the ward and actions taken on behalf of the ward, including the ward's participation in decision-making.
   e. Whether the current care plan is in the ward's best interest.
   f. Plans for future care.
   g. Recommendation as to the continuation of the guardianship and any changes needed in the guardianship order.

3) In addition, the court may appoint a visitor to review a report, interview the ward or guardian, and make any other investigation the court directs.

Changing or Terminating Guardianship

Once a guardian is appointed, it may be possible to change the guardian or terminate the guardianship. Supportive documentation is needed for presentation to the court. Except in an emergency, a change in guardian or in the guardianship order requires that a petition be filed with the court and notice provided to the ward and interested persons.

A **temporary substitute guardian** may be appointed by the court for up to 6 months when an appointed guardian is not performing effectively.

A **successor or co-guardian** may be appointed by the court to serve immediately or upon some future event. If it is a future event, such as a vacancy, then the "Acceptance of Appointment" form must be filed by any interested party within 30 days after a vacancy occurs.

A **termination of a guardian's appointment** occurs at the time of the death of the ward or guardian, or at the time of removal of the guardian by the court due to the type of guardianship and/or specified length of the appointment. A termination may also occur if the appointed guardian is not performing effectively.

A **modification of guardianship** may be granted by the court if the extent of protection or assistance previously granted is currently excessive or insufficient, based on the ward's ability to provide for his/her support, care, education, health, and welfare. A petition for modification of a guardianship order may be submitted by the ward, the guardian, or any other person interested in the ward's welfare.

Statutes Relating to Guardianship

The statutes included in this manual are listed below:

15-14-301. Appointment and status of guardian.

15-14-304. Judicial appointment of guardian - petition.

15-14-305. Preliminaries to hearing.

15-14-306. Professional evaluation.

15-14-308. Presence and rights at hearing.

15-14-309. Notice.

15-14-310. Who may be guardian - priorities - prohibition of dual roles.

15-14-311. Findings - order of appointment.

15-14-312. Emergency guardian.

15-14-313. Temporary substitute guardian.

15-14-314. Duties of guardian.

15-14-315. Powers of guardian.

15-14-315.5. Dissolution of marriage and legal separation.

15-14-316. Rights and immunities of guardian - limitations.

15-14-317. Reports - monitoring of guardianship.

15-14-318. Termination or modification of guardianship - resignation or removal of guardian.

C.R.S. Title 15, Article 14, Part 3 Guardianship Of Incapacitated Person

15-14-301. Appointment and status of guardian.

A person becomes a guardian of an incapacitated person upon appointment by the court. The guardianship continues until terminated, without regard to the location of the guardian or ward.

15-14-304. Judicial appointment of guardian - petition.

(1) An individual or a person interested in the individual's welfare may petition for a determination of incapacity, in whole or in part, and for the appointment of a limited or unlimited guardian for the individual.

(2) The petition must set forth the petitioner's name, residence, current address if different, relationship to the respondent, and interest in the appointment and, to the extent known, state or contain the following with respect to the respondent and the relief requested:

(a) The respondent's name, age, principal residence, current street address, and, if different, the address of the dwelling in which it is proposed that the respondent will reside if the appointment is made;

(b)   (I) The name and address of the respondent's:

(A) Spouse, or if the respondent has none, an adult with whom the respondent has resided for more than six months within one year before the filing of the petition; and

(B) Adult children and parents; or

(II) If the respondent has neither spouse, adult child, nor parent, at least one of the adults nearest in kinship to the respondent who can be found with reasonable efforts;

(c) The name and address of each person responsible for care or custody of the respondent, including the respondent's treating physician;

(d) The name and address of each legal representative of the respondent;

(e) The name and address of each person nominated as guardian by the respondent;

(f) The name and address of each proposed guardian and the reason why the proposed guardian should be selected;

(g) The reason why guardianship is necessary, including a brief description of the nature and extent of the respondent's alleged incapacity;

(h) If an unlimited guardianship is requested, the reason why limited guardianship is inappropriate and, if a limited guardianship is requested, the powers to be granted to the limited guardian; and

(i) A general statement of the respondent's property with an estimate of its value, including any insurance or pension, and the source and amount of any other anticipated income or receipts.

15-14-305. Preliminaries to hearing.

(1) Upon receipt of a petition to establish a guardianship, the court shall set a date and time for hearing the petition and appoint a visitor. The duties and reporting requirements of the visitor are limited to the relief requested in the petition. The visitor must be a person who has such training as the court deems appropriate.

(2) The court shall appoint a lawyer to represent the respondent in the proceeding if:

(a) Requested by the respondent;

(b) Recommended by the visitor; or

(c) The court determines that the respondent needs representation.

(3) The visitor shall interview the respondent in person and, to the extent that the respondent is able to understand:

(a) Explain to the respondent the substance of the petition, the nature, purpose, and effect of the proceeding, the respondent's rights at the hearing, and the general powers and duties of a guardian;

(b) Determine the respondent's views about the proposed guardian, the proposed guardian's powers and duties, and the scope and duration of the proposed guardianship;

(c) Inform the respondent of the right to employ and consult with a lawyer at the respondent's own expense and the right to request a court-appointed lawyer; and

(d) Inform the respondent that all costs and expenses of the proceeding, including respondent's attorney fees, will be paid from the respondent's estate unless the court directs otherwise.

(4) In addition to the duties imposed by subsection (3) of this section, the visitor shall:

(a) Interview the petitioner and the proposed guardian;

(b) Visit the respondent's present dwelling and any dwelling in which the respondent will live, if known, if the appointment is made;

(c) Obtain information from any physician or other person who is known to have treated, advised, or assessed the respondent's relevant physical or mental condition; and

(d) Make any other investigation the court directs.

(5) The visitor shall promptly file a report in writing with the court, which must include:

(a) A recommendation as to whether a lawyer should be appointed to represent the respondent and whether a guardian ad litem should be appointed to represent the respondent's best interest;

(b) A summary of daily functions the respondent can manage without assistance, could manage with the assistance of supportive services or benefits, including use of appropriate technological assistance, and cannot manage;

(c) Recommendations regarding the appropriateness of guardianship, including whether less restrictive means of intervention are available, the type of guardianship, and, if a limited guardianship, the powers to be granted to the limited guardian;

(d) A statement of the qualifications of the proposed guardian, together with a statement as to whether the respondent approves or disapproves of:

(I) The proposed guardian;

(II) The powers and duties proposed; and

(III) The scope of the guardianship;

(e) A statement as to whether the proposed dwelling meets the respondent's individual needs;

(f) A recommendation as to whether a professional evaluation or further evaluation is necessary; and

(g) Any other matters the court directs.

15-14-306. Professional evaluation.

(1) At or before a hearing under this part 3, the court may order a professional evaluation of the respondent and shall order the evaluation if the respondent so demands. If the court orders the evaluation, the respondent must be examined by a physician, psychologist, or other individual appointed by the court who is qualified to

evaluate the respondent's alleged impairment. The examiner shall promptly file a written report with the court. Unless otherwise directed by the court, the report must contain:

> (a) A description of the nature, type, and extent of the respondent's specific cognitive and functional limitations, if any;
>
> (b) An evaluation of the respondent's mental and physical condition and, if appropriate, educational potential, adaptive behavior, and social skills;
>
> (c) A prognosis for improvement and a recommendation as to the appropriate treatment or habilitation plan; and
>
> (d) The date of any assessment or examination upon which the report is based.

15-14-308. Presence and rights at hearing.

(1) Unless excused by the court for good cause, the proposed guardian shall attend the hearing. The respondent shall attend the hearing, unless excused by the court for good cause. The respondent may present evidence and subpoena witnesses and documents; examine witnesses, including any court-appointed physician, psychologist, or other individual qualified to evaluate the alleged impairment, and the visitor; and otherwise participate in the hearing. The hearing may be held in a manner that reasonably accommodates the respondent and may be closed upon the request of the respondent or upon a showing of good cause, except that the hearing may not be closed over the objection of the respondent.

(2) Any person may request permission to participate in the proceeding. The court may grant the request, with or without hearing, upon determining that the best interest of the respondent will be served. The court may attach appropriate conditions to the participation.

(3) The petitioner shall make every reasonable effort to secure the respondent's attendance at the hearing.

15-14-309. Notice.

(1) A copy of a petition for guardianship and notice of the hearing on the petition must be served personally on the respondent. The notice must include a statement that the respondent must be physically present unless excused by the court, inform the respondent of the respondent's rights at the hearing, and include a description of the nature, purpose, and consequences of an appointment. A failure to serve the respondent with a notice substantially complying with this subsection (1) is jurisdictional and thus precludes the court from granting the petition.

(2) In a proceeding to establish a guardianship, a copy of the petition for guardianship and notice of the hearing meeting the requirements of subsection (1) of this section must be given to the persons listed in the petition. Failure to give notice under this subsection (2) is not jurisdictional and thus does not preclude the appointment of a guardian or the making of a protective order.

(3) Notice of the hearing on a petition for an order after appointment of a guardian, together with a copy of the petition, must be given to the ward, the guardian, and any other person the court directs.

(4) A guardian shall give notice of the filing of the guardian's report, together with a copy of the report, to the ward and any other person the court directs. The notice must be delivered or sent within ten days after the filing of the report.

15-14-310. Who may be guardian - priorities - prohibition of dual roles.

(1) Subject to subsection (4) of this section, the court in appointing a guardian shall consider persons otherwise qualified in the following order of priority:
  (a) A guardian, other than a temporary or emergency guardian, currently acting for the respondent in this state or elsewhere;
  (b) A person nominated as guardian by the respondent, including the respondent's specific nomination of a guardian made in a durable power of attorney;
  (c) An agent appointed by the respondent under a medical durable power of attorney pursuant to section 15-14-506;
  (d) An agent appointed by the respondent under a general durable power of attorney;
  (e) The spouse of the respondent or a person nominated by will or other signed writing of a deceased spouse;
  (f) An adult child of the respondent;
  (g) A parent of the respondent or an individual nominated by will or other signed writing of a deceased parent; and
  (h) An adult with whom the respondent has resided for more than six months immediately before the filing of the petition.

(2) A respondent's nomination or appointment of a guardian shall create priority for the nominee or appointee only if, at the time of nomination or appointment, the respondent had sufficient capacity to express a preference.

(3) With respect to persons having equal priority, the court shall select the one it considers best qualified. The court, for good cause shown, may decline to appoint a person having priority and appoint a person having a lower priority or no priority.

(4) An owner, operator, or employee of a long-term-care provider from which the respondent is receiving care may not be appointed as guardian unless related to the respondent by blood, marriage, or adoption.

(5)   (a) Unless the court makes specific findings for good cause shown, the same professional may not act as an incapacitated person's or a protected person's:
        (I) Guardian and conservator; or
        (II) Guardian and direct service provider; or

(III) Conservator and direct service provider.

(b) In addition, a guardian or conservator may not employ the same person to act as both care manager and direct service provider for the incapacitated person or protected person.

15-14-311. Findings - order of appointment.

(1) The court may:
    (a) Appoint a limited or unlimited guardian for a respondent only if it finds by clear and convincing evidence that:
        (I) The respondent is an incapacitated person; and
        (II) The respondent's identified needs cannot be met by less restrictive means, including use of appropriate and reasonably available technological assistance; or
    (b) With appropriate findings, treat the petition as one for a protective order under section 15-14-401, enter any other appropriate order, or dismiss the proceeding.

(2) The court, whenever feasible, shall grant to a guardian only those powers necessitated by the ward's limitations and demonstrated needs and make appointive and other orders that will encourage the development of the ward's maximum self-reliance and independence.

(3) Within thirty days after an appointment, a guardian shall send or deliver to the ward and to all other persons given notice of the hearing on the petition a copy of the order of appointment, together with a notice of the right to request termination or modification.

15-14-312. Emergency guardian.

(1) If the court finds that compliance with the procedures of this part 3 will likely result in substantial harm to the respondent's health, safety, or welfare, and that no other person appears to have authority and willingness to act in the circumstances, the court, on petition by a person interested in the respondent's welfare, may appoint an emergency guardian whose authority may not exceed sixty days and who may exercise only the powers specified in the order. Immediately upon appointment of an emergency guardian, the court shall appoint a lawyer to represent the respondent throughout the emergency guardianship. Except as otherwise provided in subsection (2) of this section, reasonable notice of the time and place of a hearing on the petition must be given to the respondent and any other persons as the court directs.

(2) An emergency guardian may be appointed without notice to the respondent and the respondent's lawyer only if the court finds from testimony that the respondent will be substantially harmed if the appointment is delayed. If not present at the hearing, the respondent must be given notice of the appointment within forty-eight hours after the appointment. The court shall hold a hearing on the appropriateness of the appointment within ten days after the court's receipt of such a request.

(3) Appointment of an emergency guardian, with or without notice, is not a determination of the respondent's incapacity.

(4) The court may remove an emergency guardian or modify the powers granted at any time. An emergency guardian shall make any report the court requires. In other respects, the provisions of parts 1 to 4 of this article concerning guardians apply to an emergency guardian.

15-14-313. Temporary substitute guardian.

(1) If the court finds that a guardian is not effectively performing the guardian's duties and that the welfare of the ward requires immediate action, it may appoint a temporary substitute guardian for the ward for a specified period not exceeding six months. Except as otherwise ordered by the court, a temporary substitute guardian so appointed has the powers set forth in the previous order of appointment. The authority of any unlimited or limited guardian previously appointed by the court is suspended as long as a temporary substitute guardian has authority. If an appointment is made without previous notice to the ward, the affected guardian, and other interested persons, the temporary substitute guardian, within five days after the appointment, shall inform them of the appointment.

(2) The court may remove a temporary substitute guardian or modify the powers granted at any time. A temporary substitute guardian shall make any report the court requires. In other respects, the provisions of parts 1 to 4 of this article concerning guardians apply to a temporary substitute guardian.

15-14-314. Duties of guardian.

(1) Except as otherwise limited by the court, a guardian shall make decisions regarding the ward's support, care, education, health, and welfare. A guardian shall exercise authority only as necessitated by the ward's limitations and, to the extent possible, shall encourage the ward to participate in decisions, act on the ward's own behalf, and develop or regain the capacity to manage the ward's personal affairs. A guardian, in making decisions, shall consider the expressed desires and personal values of the ward to the extent known to the guardian. A guardian, at all times, shall act in the ward's best interest and exercise reasonable care, diligence, and prudence.

(2) A guardian shall:
    (a) Become or remain personally acquainted with the ward and maintain sufficient contact with the ward to know of the ward's capacities, limitations, needs, opportunities, and physical and mental health;
    (b) Take reasonable care of the ward's personal effects and bring protective proceedings if necessary to protect the property of the ward;
    (c) Expend money of the ward that has been received by the guardian for the ward's current needs for support, care, education, health, and welfare;

(d) Conserve any excess money of the ward for the ward's future needs, but if a conservator has been appointed for the estate of the ward, the guardian shall pay the money to the conservator, at least quarterly, to be conserved for the ward's future needs;

(e) Immediately notify the court if the ward's condition has changed so that the ward is capable of exercising rights previously removed;

(f) Inform the court of any change in the ward's custodial dwelling or address; and

(g) Immediately notify the court in writing of the ward's death.

15-14-315. Powers of guardian.

(1) Subject to the limitations set forth in section 15-14-316 and except as otherwise limited by the court, a guardian may:

(a) Apply for and receive money payable to the ward or the ward's guardian or custodian for the support of the ward under the terms of any statutory system of benefits or insurance or any private contract, devise, trust, conservatorship, or custodianship;

(b) If otherwise consistent with the terms of any order by a court of competent jurisdiction relating to custody of the ward, take custody of the ward and establish the ward's place of custodial dwelling, but may only establish or move the ward's place of dwelling outside this state upon express authorization of the court;

(c) If a conservator for the estate of the ward has not been appointed with existing authority, commence a proceeding, including an administrative proceeding, or take other appropriate action to compel a person to support the ward or to pay money for the benefit of the ward;

(d) Consent to medical or other care, treatment, or service for the ward; and

(e) If reasonable under all of the circumstances, delegate to the ward certain responsibilities for decisions affecting the ward's well-being.

(2) The court may specifically authorize or direct the guardian to consent to the adoption or marriage of the ward.

15-14-315.5. Dissolution of marriage and legal separation.

(1) The guardian may petition the court for authority to commence and maintain an action for dissolution of marriage or legal separation on behalf of the ward. The court may grant such authority only if satisfied, after notice and hearing, that:

(a) It is in the best interest of the ward based on evidence of abandonment, abuse, exploitation, or other compelling circumstances, and the ward either is incapable of consenting; or

(b) The ward has consented to the proposed dissolution of marriage or legal separation.

(2) Nothing in this section shall be construed as modifying the statutory grounds for dissolution of marriage and legal separation as set forth in section 14-10-106, C.R.S.

15-14-316. Rights and immunities of guardian - limitations.

(1) A guardian is entitled to reasonable compensation for services as guardian and to reimbursement for room and board provided by the guardian or one who is affiliated with the guardian, but only as approved by order of the court. If a conservator, other than the guardian or one who is affiliated with the guardian, has been appointed for the estate of the ward, reasonable compensation and reimbursement to the guardian may be approved and paid by the conservator without order of the court.

(2) A guardian need not use the guardian's personal funds for the ward's expenses. A guardian is not liable to a third person for acts of the ward solely by reason of the relationship. A guardian who exercises reasonable care in choosing a third person providing medical or other care, treatment, or service for the ward is not liable for injury to the ward resulting from the negligent or wrongful conduct of the third party.

(3) A guardian, without authorization of the court, may not revoke a medical durable power of attorney made pursuant to section 15-14-506 of which the ward is the principal. If a medical durable power of attorney made pursuant to section 15-14-506 is in effect, absent an order of the court to the contrary, a health-care decision of the agent takes precedence over that of a guardian.

(4) A guardian may not initiate the commitment of a ward to a mental health-care institution or facility except in accordance with the state's procedure for involuntary civil commitment. To obtain hospital or institutional care and treatment for mental illness of a ward, a guardian shall proceed as provided under article 10 of title 27, C.R.S. To obtain care and treatment from an approved service agency as defined in section 27-10.5-102, C.R.S., for a ward with developmental disabilities, a guardian shall proceed under article 10.5 of title 27, C.R.S. To obtain care and treatment for alcoholism or substance abuse, a guardian shall proceed as provided under part 2 of article 1 of title 25, C.R.S. No guardian shall have the authority to consent to any such care or treatment against the will of the ward.

15-14-317. Reports - monitoring of guardianship.

(1) Within sixty days after appointment or as otherwise directed by the court, a guardian shall report to the court in writing on the condition of the ward, the guardian's personal care plan for the ward, and account for money and other assets in the guardian's possession or subject to the guardian's control. A guardian shall report at least annually thereafter and whenever ordered by the court. The annual report must state or contain:
    (a) The current mental, physical, and social condition of the ward;
    (b) The living arrangements for all addresses of the ward during the reporting period;
    (c) The medical, educational, vocational, and other services provided to the ward and the guardian's opinion as to the adequacy of the ward's care;
    (d) A summary of the guardian's visits with the ward and activities on the ward's behalf and the extent to which the ward has participated in decision-making;

(e) Whether the guardian considers the current plan for care, treatment, or habilitation to be in the ward's best interest;

(f) Plans for future care; and

(g) A recommendation as to the need for continued guardianship and any recommended changes in the scope of the guardianship.

(2) The court may appoint a visitor to review a report, interview the ward or guardian, and make any other investigation the court directs.

(3) The court shall establish a system for monitoring guardianships, including the filing and review of annual reports.

15-14-318. Termination or modification of guardianship - resignation or removal of guardian.

(1) A guardianship terminates upon the death of the ward or upon order of the court.

(2) On petition of a ward, a guardian, or another person interested in the ward's welfare, the court shall terminate a guardianship if the ward no longer meets the standard for establishing the guardianship. The court may modify the type of appointment or powers granted to the guardian if the extent of protection or assistance previously granted is currently excessive or insufficient or the ward's capacity to provide for support, care, education, health, and welfare has so changed as to warrant that action.

(3) Except as otherwise ordered by the court for good cause, the court, before terminating a guardianship, shall follow the same procedures to safeguard the rights of the ward as apply to a petition for guardianship.

(4) The court may remove a guardian or permit the guardian to resign as set forth in section 15-14-112.

Conservatorship

This section of the manual defines the terms used in conservatorship proceedings, describes the procedures involved in obtaining a conservatorship, describes the duties of a conservator, and provides information on changing conservators, when necessary. Responding to allegations of abuse of conservatorship authority and other types of authority positions is addressed in the final section of the manual.

The following terms regarding conservatorship are used in this manual:

- ➤ **"Adult"** refers to the person 18 years of age or older for whom the conservatorship is being considered before a petition for conservatorship is filed with the court.
- ➤ **"Respondent"** refers to the person for whom the conservatorship is being considered once a petition for conservatorship has been filed with the court.
- ➤ **"Protected person"** refers to the person for whom the conservatorship is granted by the court.
- ➤ **"Incapacitated"** refers to an inability to effectively receive and/or evaluate information or an inability to make and/or communicate decisions to such an extent that physical health or safety is in jeopardy.
- ➤ **"Guardian ad litem"** (GAL) is a person appointed by the court to take legal action on behalf of the respondent. The guardian ad litem is charged with representing and making recommendations that are in the respondent's best interest. (For more detailed information on GAL, read C.R.S. 15-10-403 (5), C.R.S. 15-14-115 and Rule 15, Colorado Rules of Probate Procedure.)

A **conservatorship** is a court appointment for an adult who is unable to manage financial affairs because the adult is incapacitated, missing, detained, or unable to return to the United States. The appointment of a conservator gives a person or an organization the responsibility to prevent waste or dissipation of the protected person's assets. The court will authorize **limited** or **unlimited** powers and duties to the conservator in regards to those assets. The conservator obtains or provides for the support, care, education, or welfare of the protected person within the guidelines of the conservatorship order. Conservatorship for adults in Colorado is authorized by C.R.S. Title 15, Article 14, Part 4. This statute is included at the end of this section. Instruction on accessing Colorado statutes on the Internet is located in the Resource section of the manual.

*If only a **single matter or transaction** must be handled, such as sale of property or access to an account, the court may authorize such a transaction without the appointment of a conservator.*

Procedure for Obtaining a Conservatorship

This section describes the typical procedures for obtaining conservatorships. It is advisable to consult with the county attorney regarding conservatorship issues.

Prior to the Hearing

1) A **petition for appointment** of a conservator must be filed with the district court in the county in which the adult client lives. One exception is in Denver County where the petition is filed with the probate court. A petition can be initiated by the adult, a person who is interested in the adult's estate, financial affairs, or welfare, or any person who would be adversely affected by lack of effective management of the adult's property and financial affairs.

2) There are several **fees** involved in obtaining a conservatorship. The costs and expenses will be paid from respondent's estate unless the court directs otherwise. The fees are:

   a. A filing fee for the petition
   b. A fee for the court visitor
   c. Attorney fees (including petitioner's attorney fees and fees for a court appointed attorney for the respondent)

3) The order of **priorities for appointment** as a conservator follows: (In cases where two persons have equal priority, the court can select the person it considers best qualified.)

   a. Current conservator, guardian of the estate, or similar fiduciary appointed elsewhere
   b. Respondent's nominee, if he/she has sufficient capacity to express a preference at the time of nomination
   c. Agent under a durable power of attorney appointed to manage property
   d. Spouse of the respondent
   e. Adult child of the respondent
   f. Parent of the respondent
   g. Adult with whom the respondent has resided for more than 6 months immediately before the petition is filed

4) **The court may prohibit some persons or service providers from dual appointments** due to concerns regarding dual role conflicts. However, the court may make an exception for good cause. Examples of persons who may be excluded from consideration as conservator due to a dual role conflict are:

a. Long-term care providers unless related by blood, marriage, or adoption
b. Paid professionals who are serving a protected person as either guardian or direct service provider
c. Persons employed as both care manager and direct service provider for a protected person

5) A **court visitor** is assigned by the court to act as an investigator for the court. The duties and reporting requirements of the visitor are limited to those requested in the petition.

a. The visitor must interview:
   - The respondent
   - The proposed conservator
   - Any other party the court directs
b. The visitor must explain to the respondent:
   - The substance of the petition
   - The nature, purpose, and effect of the proceeding
   - The respondent's rights to an attorney at the respondent's own expense or right to a court-appointed attorney
   - General powers and duties of a conservator
   - That costs and expenses will be paid from respondent's estate unless the court directs otherwise
c. The visitor must determine the respondent's views about:
   - The proposed conservator
   - The conservator's powers and duties
   - The scope and duration of conservatorship
d. Once the investigation is complete, the visitor must file a written report with the court which includes:
   - A recommendation as to whether an attorney or guardian ad litem should be appointed
   - A recommendation as to the appropriateness of conservatorship, the type of conservatorship that should be granted, and if limited, the powers and duties to be granted
   - A recommendation as to whether further evaluation or a professional evaluation of the respondent is necessary
   - A statement about qualifications of the conservator and the respondent's views of the conservator

6) The court may **appoint an attorney** if requested by the respondent, recommended by the court visitor, or if the court determines it necessary.

7) The court may appoint a physician, psychologist, or other qualified individual to conduct a **professional (functional) evaluation** of the respondent.

8) While the petition is pending, the court may issue an order to apply the property of the respondent for the **support of the respondent** or other dependents.

9) Once a petition has been filed, a **notice of the hearing** must be *personally* served on the respondent. The notice must be sent to all interested persons named in the petition.

   a. Interested persons may include, but are not limited to:
      - Respondent's spouse
      - Respondent's adult children
      - Respondent's parents
      - Each person responsible for the care or custody of the respondent
      - Treating physician of the respondent
      - Each legal representative of the respondent
      - Each person nominated as a conservator by the respondent
   b. The "Notice of Hearing on the Petition" must be served:
      - At least 10 days prior to the hearing
      - By any person who does not have an interest in the outcome of the conservatorship proceeding (It is not necessary to hire a process server.)
   c. The notice must include:
      - A copy of the petition
      - A statement that the respondent must be physically present at the hearing unless excused by the court
      - Information about the respondent's rights at hearing
      - A description of the nature, purpose, and consequences of a conservator appointment

Hearing Procedures

10) The conservatorship statute stipulates the **respondent's rights at the hearing**. The respondent has the right to:

    a. Have notice of, and be present at, the hearing
    b. Have representation by counsel of choice at the respondent's expense or have right to a court appointed attorney
    c. Present evidence
    d. Subpoena witnesses and documents and examine witnesses, including the court visitor, any evaluator, physician, or psychologist

11) The conservatorship statute clarifies **where and how the hearing may be conducted**.

    a. The respondent must attend the hearing unless excused by the court for good cause. (The court may hold the hearing in a manner that reasonably accommodates the respondent, such as by telephone or at the respondent's place of residence.)

b. The petitioner and proposed conservator (if different) must attend unless excused by the court for good cause.
c. Any person may request permission to participate in the proceedings
d. The hearing is open to the public, unless closed at the request of the respondent or any interested party showing good cause.
e. The hearing cannot be closed over the objections of the respondent.

Following the Hearing

12) A decision by the court to grant conservatorship will be made as necessitated by the protected person's limitations and demonstrated needs. The court will enter the least restrictive order that encourages the development of maximum self-reliance and independence of the protected person.

13) A conservator must give **notice of the conservatorship appointment** within 30 days after an appointment to the protected person and all other persons who were given notice of the original petition. The notice will include a copy of the:

   a. Notice of appointment and right to request termination or modification
   b. Court order

14) The conservator must file a **financial plan** with the court within 90 days of appointment. A notice of filing of the financial plan, including copies of all pertinent documents, must be sent to the respondent and all others listed on the original petition within 10 days of filing the report with the court. This financial plan must include a:

   a. Comparison of projected income and expenses
   b. Plan to address the needs of the protected person
   c. Plan of management for the estate
   d. Detailed inventory of the estate

Duties and Powers of a Conservator

A conservator is expected to understand and carry out the responsibilities outlined in the specific conservatorship orders. When in doubt about the authority to decide on a specific matter, a conservator should seek prior approval from the court. While individual conservatorship orders may contain specific instructions, there are general duties and responsibilities, which every conservator is expected to fulfill.

1) The conservator must furnish a bond, unless waived by the court for good cause, to protect cash and other assets, or take other steps to safeguard the protected person's assets. The bond requirement will be specified in the order appointing the conservator and filed with the court.

2) The conservator is required to file an annual report with the court which must include:

   a. A list of assets of the estate, receipts, disbursements, and distributions during the period of the report
   b. Documentation of services provided to the protected person
   c. Recommended changes in the financial plan
   d. Recommended changes in the scope of the conservatorship

3) In general, a conservator's powers include all powers over the estate and affairs the protected person could exercise if not under conservatorship. The powers of a conservator include but are not limited to:

   a. Making gifts
   b. Conveying, releasing, and disclaiming interests
   c. Creating, revoking, or amending trusts
   d. Exercising rights and changing beneficiaries under retirement plans, insurance, and annuities
   e. Exercising rights to elective shares of stock
   f. Making, amending, or revoking the protected person's will

4) Conservators are entitled to reasonable compensation payable from the protected person's estate.

   a. Family members usually do *not* receive compensation.
   b. Family members *do* receive reimbursement of expenses.

Changing and Terminating Conservatorship

Once a conservator is appointed, it is possible to change the conservator or terminate the conservatorship. Supportive documentation and appropriate forms will be needed for presentation to the court.

A **special conservator** may be appointed by the court as a temporary or successor conservator when the original conservator is not performing effectively or other circumstances keep the conservator from performing his/her duties. Additionally, a special conservator can be appointed to assist the original conservator with an authorized project.

To request a special conservator appointment, a petition requesting a conservator must be filed and an "Order Appointing Special Conservator" form will need to be completed. Information on accessing forms related to conservatorship is found in the Resource section of this manual.

If there is cause to **terminate the conservatorship** of a protected person, an order terminating conservatorship may be entered by the court. For adults, reasons for termination of conservatorship may include but are not limited to:

- The disability or impairment of the protected person ended.
- The protected person died.
- There are insufficient assets of the estate to warrant continued administration.

Statutes Relating to Conservatorship

The statutes included in this manual are listed below:

C.R.S. Title 15, Article 14, Part 4 Protection Of Property Of Protected Person

15-14-401. Protective proceeding.

(1) Upon petition and after notice and hearing, the court may appoint a limited or unlimited conservator or make any other protective order provided in this part 4 in relation to the estate and affairs of:

(a) A minor, if the court determines that the minor owns money or property requiring management or protection that cannot otherwise be provided or has or may have business affairs that may be put at risk or prevented because of the minor's age, or that money is needed for support and education and that protection is necessary or desirable to obtain or provide money; or

(b) Any individual, including a minor, if the court determines that, for reasons other than age:

(I) By clear and convincing evidence, the individual is unable to manage property and business affairs because the individual is unable to effectively receive or evaluate information or both or to make or communicate decisions, even with the use of appropriate and reasonably available technological assistance, or because the individual is missing, detained, or unable to return to the United States; and

(II) By a preponderance of evidence, the individual has property that will be wasted or dissipated unless management is provided or money is needed for the support, care, education, health, and welfare of the individual or of individuals who are entitled to the individual's support and that protection is necessary or desirable to obtain or provide money.

15-14-402. Jurisdiction over business affairs of protected person.

(1) After the service of notice in a proceeding seeking a conservatorship or other protective order and until termination of the proceeding, the court in which the petition is filed has:

(a) Exclusive jurisdiction to determine the need for a conservatorship or other protective order;

(b) Exclusive jurisdiction to determine how the estate of the protected person which is subject to the laws of this state must be managed, expended, or distributed to or for the use of the protected person, individuals who are in fact dependent upon the protected person, or other claimants; and

(c) Concurrent jurisdiction to determine the validity of claims against the person or estate of the protected person and questions of title concerning assets of the estate.

15-14-403. Original petition for appointment or protective order.

(1) The following may petition for the appointment of a conservator or for any other appropriate protective order:

(a) The person to be protected;

(b) An individual interested in the estate, affairs, or welfare of the person to be protected, including a parent, guardian, or custodian; or

(c) A person who would be adversely affected by lack of effective management of the property and business affairs of the person to be protected.

(2) A petition under subsection (1) of this section must set forth the petitioner's name, residence, current address if different, relationship to the respondent, and interest in the appointment or other protective order, and, to the extent known, state or contain the following with respect to the respondent and the relief requested:

(a) The respondent's name, age, principal residence, current street address, and, if different, the address of the dwelling where it is proposed that the respondent will reside if the appointment is made;

(b) If the petition alleges impairment in the respondent's ability to effectively receive and evaluate information, a brief description of the nature and extent of the respondent's alleged impairment;

(c) If the petition alleges that the respondent is missing, detained, or unable to return to the United States, a statement of the relevant circumstances, including the time and nature of the disappearance or detention and a description of any search or inquiry concerning the respondent's whereabouts;

(d)   (I) The name and address of the respondent's:

(A) Spouse or, if the respondent has none, an adult with whom the respondent has resided for more than six months within one year before the filing of the petition; and

(B) Adult children and parents; or

(II) If the respondent has neither spouse, adult child, nor parent, at least one of the adults nearest in kinship to the respondent who can be found with reasonable efforts;

(e) The name and address of each person responsible for care or custody of the respondent, including the respondent's treating physician;

(f) The name and address of each legal representative of the respondent;

(g) A general statement of the respondent's property with an estimate of its value, including any insurance or pension, and the source and amount of other anticipated income or receipts; and

(h) The reason why a conservatorship or other protective order is in the best interest of the respondent.

(3) If a conservatorship is requested, the petition must also set forth to the extent known:

(a) The name and address of each proposed conservator and the reason why the proposed conservator should be selected;

(b) The name and address of each person nominated as conservator by the respondent if the respondent has attained twelve years of age; and

(c) The type of conservatorship requested and, if an unlimited conservatorship, the reason why limited conservatorship is inappropriate or, if a limited conservatorship, the property to be placed under the conservator's control and any limitation on the conservator's powers and duties.

15-14-404. Notice.

(1) A copy of the petition and the notice of hearing on a petition for conservatorship or other protective order must be served personally on the respondent, if the respondent has attained twelve years of age, but if the respondent's whereabouts are unknown or personal service cannot be made, service on the respondent must be made by substituted service or publication. The notice must include a statement that the respondent must be physically present unless excused by the court, inform the respondent of the respondent's rights at the hearing, and, if the appointment of a conservator is requested, include a description of the nature, purpose, and consequences of an appointment. A failure to serve the respondent with a notice substantially complying with this subsection (1) is jurisdictional and thus precludes the court from granting the petition.

(2) In a proceeding to establish a conservatorship or for another protective order, notice of the hearing must be given to the persons listed in the petition. Failure to give notice under this subsection (2) does not preclude the appointment of a conservator or the making of another protective order.

(3) Notice of the hearing on a petition for an order after appointment of a conservator or making of another protective order, together with a copy of the petition, must be given to the protected person, if the protected person has attained twelve years of age and is not missing, detained, or unable to return to the United States, any conservator of the protected person's estate, and any other person as ordered by the court.

(4) A conservator shall give notice of the filing of the conservator's inventory, report, or plan of conservatorship, together with a copy of the inventory, report, or plan of conservatorship to the protected person and any other person the court directs. The notice must be delivered or sent within ten days after the filing of the inventory, report, or plan of conservatorship.

15-14-406. Original petition - persons under disability - preliminaries to hearing.

(1) Upon the filing of a petition for a conservatorship or other protective order for a respondent for reasons other than being a minor, the court shall set a date for hearing. The court shall appoint a visitor unless the petition does not request the appointment of a conservator and the respondent is represented by a lawyer. The duties and reporting requirements of the visitor are limited to the relief requested in the petition. The visitor must be a person who has such training or experience as the court deems appropriate.

(2) The court shall appoint a lawyer to represent the respondent in the proceeding if:
    (a) Requested by the respondent;

(b) Recommended by the visitor; or

(c) The court determines that the respondent needs representation.

(3) The visitor shall interview the respondent in person and, to the extent that the respondent is able to understand:

(a) Explain to the respondent the substance of the petition and the nature, purpose, and effect of the proceeding;

(b) If the appointment of a conservator is requested, inform the respondent of the general powers and duties of a conservator and determine the respondent's views regarding the proposed conservator, the proposed conservator's powers and duties, and the scope and duration of the proposed conservatorship;

(c) Inform the respondent of the respondent's rights, including the right to employ and consult with a lawyer at the respondent's own expense, and the right to request a court-appointed lawyer; and

(d) Inform the respondent that all costs and expenses of the proceeding, including respondent's attorney fees, will be paid from the respondent's estate unless the court directs otherwise.

(4) In addition to the duties imposed by subsection (3) of this section, the visitor shall:

(a) Interview the petitioner and the proposed conservator, if any; and

(b) Make any other investigation the court directs.

(5) The visitor shall promptly file a report with the court, which must include:

(a) A recommendation as to whether a lawyer should be appointed to represent the respondent and whether a guardian ad litem should be appointed to represent the respondent's best interest;

(b) Recommendations regarding the appropriateness of a conservatorship, including whether less restrictive means of intervention are available, the type of conservatorship, and, if a limited conservatorship, the powers and duties to be granted the limited conservator, and the assets over which the conservator should be granted authority;

(c) A statement of the qualifications of the proposed conservator, together with a statement as to whether the respondent approves or disapproves of:

(I) The proposed conservator;

(II) The powers and duties proposed; and

(III) The scope of the conservatorship;

(d) A recommendation as to whether a professional evaluation or further evaluation is necessary; and

(e) Any other matters the court directs.

(6) The court may also appoint a physician, psychologist, or other individual qualified to evaluate the alleged impairment to conduct an examination of the respondent.

(7) While a petition to establish a conservatorship or for another protective order is pending, after preliminary hearing and without notice to others, the court may issue orders to preserve and apply the property of the respondent as may be required for the

support of the respondent or individuals who are in fact dependent upon the respondent. The court may appoint a special conservator to assist in that task.

15-14-408. Original petition - procedure at hearing.

(1) Unless excused by the court for good cause, a proposed conservator shall attend the hearing. The respondent shall attend the hearing, unless excused by the court for good cause. The respondent may present evidence and subpoena witnesses and documents, examine witnesses, including any court-appointed physician, psychologist, or other individual qualified to evaluate the alleged impairment, and the visitor, and otherwise participate in the hearing. The hearing may be held in a manner that reasonably accommodates the respondent and may be closed upon request of the respondent, or upon a showing of good cause; except that the hearing may not be closed over the objection of the respondent.

(2) Any person may request permission to participate in the proceeding. The court may grant the request, with or without hearing, upon determining that the best interest of the respondent will be served. The court may attach appropriate conditions to the participation.

(3) The petitioner shall make every reasonable effort to secure the respondent's attendance at the hearing.

15-14-409. Original petition - orders.

(1) If a proceeding is brought for the reason that the respondent is a minor, after a hearing on the petition, upon finding that the appointment of a conservator or other protective order is in the best interest of the minor, the court shall make an appointment or other appropriate protective order.

(2) If a proceeding is brought for reasons other than that the respondent is a minor, after a hearing on the petition, upon finding that a basis exists for a conservatorship or other protective order, the court shall make the least restrictive order consistent with its findings. The court shall make orders necessitated by the protected person's limitations and demonstrated needs, including appointive and other orders that will encourage the development of maximum self-reliance and independence of the protected person.

(3) Within thirty days after an appointment, the conservator shall deliver or send a copy of the order of appointment, together with a statement of the right to seek termination or modification, to the protected person, if the protected person has attained twelve years of age and is not missing, detained, or unable to return to the United States, and to all other persons given notice of the petition.

(4) The appointment of a conservator or the entry of another protective order is not a determination of incapacity of the protected person.

15-14-410. Powers of court.

(1) After hearing and upon determining that a basis for a conservatorship or other protective order exists, the court has the following powers, which may be exercised directly or through a conservator:
> (a) With respect to a minor for reasons of age, all the powers over the estate and business affairs of the minor that may be necessary for the best interest of the minor and members of the minor's immediate family; and
> (b) With respect to an adult, or to a minor for reasons other than age, for the benefit of the protected person and individuals who are in fact dependent on the protected person for support, all the powers over the estate and business affairs of the protected person that the person could exercise if the person were an adult, present, and not under conservatorship or other protective order.

(2) Subject to section 15-14-110 requiring endorsement of limitations on the letters of office, the court may limit at any time the powers of a conservator otherwise conferred and may remove or modify any limitation.

15-14-411. Required court approval.

(1) After notice to interested persons and upon express authorization of the court, a conservator may:
> (a) Make gifts, except as otherwise provided in section 15-14-427 (2);
> (b) Convey, release, or disclaim contingent and expectant interests in property, including marital property rights and any right of survivorship incident to joint tenancy or tenancy by the entireties;
> (c) Exercise or release a power of appointment;
> (d) Create a revocable or irrevocable trust of property of the estate, whether or not the trust extends beyond the duration of the conservatorship, or revoke or amend a trust revocable by the protected person;
> (e) Exercise rights to elect options and change beneficiaries under retirement plans, insurance policies, and annuities or surrender the plans, policies, and annuities for their cash value;
> (f) Exercise any right to an elective share in the estate of the protected person's deceased spouse and to renounce or disclaim any interest by testate or intestate succession or by transfer inter vivos; and
> (g) Make, amend, or revoke the protected person's will.

(2) A conservator, in making, amending, or revoking the protected person's will, shall comply with section 15-11-502 or 15-11-507.

(3) The court, in exercising or in approving a conservator's exercise of the powers listed in subsection (1) of this section, shall consider primarily the decision that the protected person would have made, to the extent that the decision can be ascertained. To the extent the decision cannot be ascertained, the court shall consider the best interest of the protected person. The court shall also consider:

(a) The financial needs of the protected person and the needs of individuals who are in fact dependent on the protected person for support and the interest of creditors;

(b) Possible reduction of income, estate, inheritance, or other tax liabilities;

(c) Eligibility for governmental assistance;

(d) The protected person's previous pattern of giving or level of support;

(e) The existing estate plan;

(f) The protected person's life expectancy and the probability that the conservatorship will terminate before the protected person's death; and

(g) Any other factors the court considers relevant, including the best interest of the protected person.

15-14-412. Protective arrangements and single transactions.

(1) If a basis is established for a protective order with respect to an individual, the court, without appointing a conservator, may:

(a) Authorize, direct, or ratify any transaction necessary or desirable to achieve any arrangement for security, service, or care meeting the foreseeable needs of the protected person, including:

(I) Payment, delivery, deposit, or retention of funds or property;

(II) Sale, mortgage, lease, or other transfer of property;

(III) Purchase of an annuity;

(IV) Making a contract for life care, deposit contract, or contract for training and education; or

(V) Addition to or establishment of a suitable trust, including a trust created under the "Colorado Uniform Custodial Trust Act", article 1.5 of this title; and

(b) Authorize, direct, or ratify any other contract, trust, will, or transaction relating to the protected person's property and business affairs, including a settlement of, and distribution of settlement of, a claim, upon determining that it is in the best interest of the protected person.

(2) In deciding whether to approve a protective arrangement or other transaction under this section, the court shall consider the factors described in section 15-14-411 (3).

(3) The court may appoint a special conservator to assist in the accomplishment of any protective arrangement or other transaction authorized under this section. The special conservator has the authority conferred by the order and shall serve until discharged by order after report to the court.

15-14-413. Who may be conservator - priorities - prohibition of dual roles.

(1) Except as otherwise provided in subsection (4) of this section, the court, in appointing a conservator, shall consider persons otherwise qualified in the following order of priority:

(a) A conservator, guardian of the estate, or other like fiduciary appointed or recognized by an appropriate court of any other jurisdiction in which the protected person resides;

(b) A person nominated as conservator by the respondent, including the respondent's specific nomination of a conservator made in a durable power of attorney, if the respondent has attained twelve years of age;

(c) An agent appointed by the respondent to manage the respondent's property under a durable power of attorney;

(d) The spouse of the respondent;

(e) An adult child of the respondent;

(f) A parent of the respondent; and

(g) An adult with whom the respondent has resided for more than six months immediately before the filing of the petition.

(2) A respondent's nomination or appointment of a conservator shall create priority for the nominee or appointee only if, at the time of nomination or appointment, the respondent had sufficient capacity to express a preference.

(3) A person having priority under paragraph (a), (d), (e), or (f) of subsection (1) of this section may designate in writing a substitute to serve instead and thereby transfer the priority to the substitute.

(4) With respect to persons having equal priority, the court shall select the one it considers best qualified. The court, for good cause, may decline to appoint a person having priority and appoint a person having a lower priority or no priority.

(5) An owner, operator, or employee of a long-term care provider from which the respondent is receiving care may not be appointed as conservator unless related to the respondent by blood, marriage, or adoption.

(6)   (a) Unless the court makes specific findings for good cause shown, the same professional may not act as an incapacitated person's or a protected person's:

    (I) Guardian and conservator; or
    (II) Guardian and direct service provider; or
    (III) Conservator and direct service provider.

(b) In addition, a guardian or conservator may not employ the same person to act as both care manager and direct service provider for the incapacitated person or protected person.

15-14-414. Petition for order subsequent to appointment.

(1) A protected person or a person interested in the welfare of a protected person may file a petition in the appointing court for an order:

(a) Requiring bond or collateral or additional bond or collateral, or reducing bond or collateral;

(b) Requiring an accounting for the administration of the protected person's estate;

(c) Directing distribution;

(d) Removing the conservator and appointing a temporary or successor conservator;

(e) Modifying the type of appointment or powers granted to the conservator if the extent of protection or management previously granted is currently excessive or insufficient or the protected person's ability to manage the estate and business affairs has so changed as to warrant the action; or

(f) Granting other appropriate relief.

(2) A conservator may petition the appointing court for instructions concerning fiduciary responsibility.

(3) Upon notice and hearing the petition, the court may give appropriate instructions and make any appropriate order.

(4) At the conclusion of the hearings authorized by this section, the court may review the motions and petitions filed by a party under this section to determine if they were substantially warranted and brought in good faith. If, after the hearing, the court determines that the motions and petitions filed under this section were not substantially warranted or were brought in bad faith, the court may award fees and costs against the movant or petitioner including, but not limited to, the attorney fees and costs incurred by the conservatorship, or the affected parties, in responding to the motions and petitions.

15-14-415. Bond.

Unless the court makes specific findings as to the reasons a bond is not required in the present case, the court shall require a conservator to furnish a bond conditioned upon faithful discharge of all duties of the conservatorship according to law, with sureties as it may specify. In the alternative, the court may impose restrictions upon the conservator's access to, or transfer of, the assets of the conservatorship estate. Unless otherwise directed by the court, the cost of the bond shall be charged to the protected person's estate and the bond must be in the amount of the aggregate capital value of the property of the estate in the conservator's control, plus one year's estimated income, and minus the value of assets deposited under arrangements requiring an order of the court for their removal and the value of any real property that the fiduciary, by express limitation, lacks power to sell or convey without court authorization. The court, in place of sureties on a bond, may accept collateral for the performance of the bond, including a pledge of securities or a mortgage of real property.

15-14-416. Terms and requirements of bond.

(1) The following rules apply to any bond required:

(a) Except as otherwise provided by the terms of the bond, sureties and the conservator are jointly and severally liable.

(b) By executing the bond of a conservator, a surety submits to the jurisdiction of the court that issued letters to the primary obligor in any proceeding pertaining to the fiduciary duties of the conservator in which the surety is named as a party. Notice of any proceeding must be sent or delivered to the surety at the address shown in the court records at the place where the bond is filed and to any other address then known to the petitioner.

(c) On petition of a successor conservator or any interested person, a proceeding may be brought against a surety for breach of the obligation of the bond of the conservator.

(d) The bond of the conservator may be proceeded against until liability under the bond is exhausted.

(e) Unless otherwise directed by the court, the cost of the bond shall be paid from the protected person's estate.

(2) A proceeding may not be brought against a surety on any matter as to which an action or proceeding against the primary obligor is barred.

(3) If there is a request for the waiver or reduction of a surety upon a bond, the court may require the conservator to supply the court with a credit report, a statement of the conservator's assets, liabilities, income, and expenses, and a statement about any interests the conservator may have in or liability to the conservatorship estate, or any other information the court may wish to consider.

15-14-417. Compensation, fees, costs, and expenses of administration - expenses.

(1) Compensation. If not otherwise compensated for services rendered, any visitor, guardian, conservator, special conservator, lawyer for the respondent, lawyer whose services resulted in a protective order or in an order beneficial to an incapacitated person or to a protected person's estate, any physician, guardian ad litem, or any other person appointed by the court is entitled to reasonable compensation from the estate even if no fiduciary is appointed. Except as limited by court order, compensation may be paid and expenses reimbursed without court order. In a special conservatorship, compensation may only be paid with court approval after notice and hearing. If the court determines that the compensation is excessive or the expenses are inappropriate, the excessive or inappropriate amount must be repaid to the estate.

(2) Fees. Factors to be considered as guides in determining the reasonableness of any fee referred to in this section or in this article or in article 16 of this title, include the following:

(a) The time and labor required, the novelty and difficulty of the questions involved, and the skill requisite to perform the service properly;

(b) The likelihood, if apparent, that the acceptance of the particular employment will preclude the person employed from other employment;

(c) The fee customarily charged in the locality for similar services;

(d) The amount involved and the results obtained;

(e) The time limitations imposed by the circumstances;

(f) The experience, reputation, and ability of the person performing the services.

(3) Expenses in estate litigation. For purposes of this article or article 16 of this title, if any guardian, conservator, special conservator, or court-appointed fiduciary defends or prosecutes any proceeding in good faith, whether successful or not, he or she is entitled to receive from the estate his or her necessary time, expenses, and disbursements including reasonable attorney fees incurred. Any such person or fiduciary who is unsuccessful in defending the propriety of his or her actions in a breach of fiduciary duty action shall not be entitled to recover expenses under this section to the extent of any matters on which such breaches are found.

(4) Expenses incurred in defense of fiduciary fees. For purposes of this article and article 16 of this title, if any fiduciary is required to defend his or her fees or costs, at the end of the proceedings, the court shall consider the fees and expenses incurred by the fiduciary in a fee review. The court has the authority and duty to determine whether to award to the fiduciary the fiduciary's own fees and costs, including the fiduciary's own attorney fees and costs, incurred in the defense of the fiduciary's fees and costs as the court deems equitable under the circumstances of the case. Any award of fees or costs to the fiduciary may be ordered paid from, and may be allocated among, the estate or trust, or from the person, party, or organization that required the fiduciary to defend his or her fees or costs, as the court deems just.

(5) Priority for payment of guardianship or conservatorship costs and expenses of administration after the death of the incapacitated person or protected person. When an incapacitated person or a protected person dies, all fees, costs, and expenses of administration of the guardianship or conservatorship including any unpaid guardian or conservator fees and costs and those of their counsel may be submitted to the court for court approval in conjunction with the termination of the guardianship or conservatorship estate. Thereafter, all court-approved fees, costs, and expenses of administration arising from the guardianship or conservatorship shall be paid as court-approved claims for costs and expenses of administration in the decedent's estate. In the event that there are insufficient funds to pay all claims in the decedent's estate in full, the fees, costs, and expenses of administration arising from the guardianship or conservatorship shall retain their classification as "costs and expenses of administration" in the decedent's estate and shall be paid pursuant to section 15-12-805.

(6) A fiduciary who is a member of a law firm may use that law firm and charge for the legal services of the members and staff of that firm to assist the fiduciary in his or her duties as a fiduciary.

15-14-418. General duties of conservator - financial plan.

(1) A conservator, in relation to powers conferred by this part 4 or implicit in the title acquired by virtue of the proceeding, is a fiduciary and shall observe the standards of care applicable to a trustee.

(2) A conservator shall take into account the limitations of the protected person, and to the extent possible, as directed by the order of appointment or the financial plan, encourage the person to participate in decisions, act in the person's own behalf, and develop or regain the ability to manage the person's estate and business affairs.

(3) Within a time set by the court, but no later than ninety days after appointment, a conservator shall file for approval with the appointing court a financial plan for protecting, managing, expending, and distributing the income and assets of the protected person's estate. The financial plan shall be based upon a comparison of the projected income and expenses of the protected person and shall set forth a plan to address the needs of the person and how the assets and income of the protected person shall be managed to meet those needs. The financial plan must be based on the actual needs of the person and take into consideration the best interest of the person. The conservator shall include in the financial plan steps to the extent possible to develop or restore the person's ability to manage the person's property, an estimate of the duration of the conservatorship, and projections of expenses and resources.

(4) In investing an estate, selecting assets of the estate for distribution, and invoking powers of revocation or withdrawal available for the use and benefit of the protected person and exercisable by the conservator, a conservator shall take into account any estate plan of the person known to the conservator. The conservator may examine the will and any other donative, nominative, or other appointive instrument of the person.

(5) A conservator shall file an amended financial plan whenever there is a change in circumstances that requires a substantial deviation from the existing financial plan.

15-14-419. Inventory.

(1) Within a time set by the court, but no later than ninety days after appointment, a conservator shall prepare and file with the appointing court a detailed inventory of the estate subject to the conservatorship, together with an oath or affirmation that the inventory is believed to be complete and accurate as far as information permits.

(2) If any property not included in the original inventory comes to the knowledge of a conservator or if the conservator learns that the value or description indicated in the original inventory for any item is erroneous or misleading, he or she shall prepare an amended inventory and file it with the court and provide copies to interested parties as directed by prior court orders.

15-14-420. Reports - appointment of monitor - monitoring - records.

(1) A conservator shall report to the court about the administration of the estate annually unless the court otherwise directs. Upon filing a petition or motion and after notice, a conservator shall be entitled to a hearing to settle all matters covered in an intermediate or final report. An order, after notice and hearing, allowing an intermediate report of a

conservator adjudicates all of the conservator's, his or her other counsel's, and his or her other agent's liabilities concerning all matters adequately disclosed in the report. An order, after notice and hearing, allowing a final report adjudicates all previously unsettled liabilities of the conservator, his or her counsel, and that of his or her agents relating to the conservatorship, the protected person, or the protected person's successors.

(2) A report must:
>   (a) Contain a list of the assets of the estate under the conservator's control and a list of the receipts, disbursements, and distributions during the period for which the report is made;
>   (b) Reflect the services provided to the protected person; and
>   (c) State any recommended changes in the plan for the conservatorship as well as a recommendation as to the continued need for conservatorship and any recommended changes in the scope of the conservatorship.

(3) The court may appoint a suitable person to review a report or plan, interview the protected person or conservator, and make any other investigation the court directs. In connection with a report, the court may order a conservator to submit the assets of the estate to an appropriate examination to be made in a manner the court directs.

(4) The court shall establish a system for monitoring conservatorships, including the filing and review of conservators' reports and plans.

(5) A conservator shall keep records of the administration of the estate and make them available for examination on reasonable request of an interested person.

15-14-421. Title by appointment.

(1) Except as limited in the appointing order, the appointment of a conservator vests title in the conservator as trustee to all property of the protected person, or to the part thereof specified in the order, held at the time of appointment or thereafter acquired, including title to any property held for the protected person by custodians or attorneys-in-fact. An order vesting title in the conservator to only a part of the property of the protected person creates a conservatorship limited to assets specified in the order. Notwithstanding the language vesting title in the conservator in this section, this vesting of title shall not be construed to sever any joint tenancies.

(2) Letters of conservatorship are evidence of vesting title of the protected person's assets in the conservator. An order terminating a conservatorship transfers title to assets remaining subject to the conservatorship, including any described in the order, to the formerly protected person or the person's successors.

(3) Subject to the requirements of other statutes governing the filing or recordation of documents of title to land or other property, letters of conservatorship and orders

terminating conservatorships may be filed or recorded to give notice of title as between the conservator and the protected person.

(4) Neither the appointment of a conservator nor the establishment of a trust in accordance with section 15-14-412.5 to 15-14-412.9 is a transfer or an alienation within the meaning of the general provisions of any federal or state statute or regulation, insurance policy, pension plan, contract, will or trust instrument imposing restrictions upon or penalties for the transfer or alienation by the protected person of his or her rights or interest, but this section does not restrict the ability of a person to make specific provisions by contract or dispositive instrument relating to a conservator.

(5) Except as limited in the appointing order, a conservator has the authority to continue, modify, or revoke any financial power of attorney previously created by the protected person.

(6)   (a) Upon notice of the appointment of a conservator, all agents acting under a previously created power of attorney by the protected person shall:
           (I) Take no further actions without the direct written authorization of the conservator;
           (II) Shall promptly report to the conservator as to any action taken under the power of attorney; and
           (III) Shall promptly account to the conservator for all actions taken under the power of attorney.
        (b) Nothing in this section shall be construed to affect previously created medical decision-making authority. Any agent violating this section shall be liable to the protected person's estate for all costs incurred in attempting to obtain compliance, including but not limited to reasonable conservator and attorney fees and costs.

15-14-422. Protected person's interest inalienable.

(1) Except as otherwise provided in subsections (3) and (4) of this section, the interest of a protected person in property vested in a conservator is not transferable or assignable by the protected person. An attempted transfer or assignment by the protected person, although ineffective to affect property rights, may give rise to a claim against the protected person for restitution or damages that, subject to presentation and allowance, may be satisfied as provided in section 15-14-429.

(2) Property vested in a conservator by appointment and the interest of the protected person in that property are not subject to levy, garnishment, or similar process for claims against the protected person unless allowed under section 15-14-429.

(3) A person without knowledge of the conservatorship who in good faith and for security or substantially equivalent value receives delivery from a protected person of tangible personal property of a type normally transferred by delivery of possession, is protected as if the protected person or transferee had valid title.

(4) A third party who deals with the protected person with respect to property vested in a conservator is entitled to any protection provided in other law.

15-14-423. Sale, encumbrance, or other transaction involving conflict of interest.

Any transaction involving the conservatorship estate that is affected by a substantial conflict between the conservator's fiduciary and personal interests is voidable unless the transaction is expressly authorized by the court after notice to interested persons. A transaction affected by a substantial conflict between personal and fiduciary interests includes any sale, encumbrance, or other transaction involving the conservatorship estate entered into by the conservator, the spouse, descendant, agent, or lawyer of a conservator, or a corporation or other enterprise in which the conservator has a substantial beneficial interest.

15-14-424. Protection of person dealing with conservator.

(1) A person who assists or deals with a conservator in good faith and for value in any transaction other than one requiring a court order under section 15-14-410 or 15-14-411 is protected as though the conservator properly exercised the power. That a person knowingly deals with a conservator does not alone require the person to inquire into the existence of a power or the propriety of its exercise, but restrictions on powers of conservators that are endorsed on letters as provided in section 15-14-110 are effective as to third persons. A person who pays or delivers assets to a conservator is not responsible for their proper application.

(2) Protection provided by this section extends to any procedural irregularity or jurisdictional defect that occurred in proceedings leading to the issuance of letters and is not a substitute for protection provided to persons assisting or dealing with a conservator by comparable provisions in other law relating to commercial transactions or to simplifying transfers of securities by fiduciaries.

(3) Any recorded instrument evidencing a transaction described in this section on which a state documentary fee is noted pursuant to section 39-13-103, C.R.S., shall be prima facie evidence that such transaction was made for value.

15-14-425. Powers of conservator in administration.

(1) Except as otherwise qualified or limited by the court in its order of appointment and endorsed on the letters, a conservator has all of the powers granted in this section and any additional powers granted by law to a trustee in this state.

(2) A conservator, acting reasonably and in an effort to accomplish the purpose of the appointment, and without further court authorization or confirmation, may:

(a) Collect, hold, and retain assets of the estate, including assets in which the conservator has a personal interest and real property in another state, until the conservator considers that disposition of an asset should be made;

(b) Receive additions to the estate;

(c) Continue or participate in the operation of any business or other enterprise;

(d) Acquire an undivided interest in an asset of the estate in which the conservator, in any fiduciary capacity, holds an undivided interest;

(e) Invest assets of the estate as though the conservator were a trustee;

(f) Deposit money of the estate in a financial institution, including one operated by the conservator;

(g) Acquire or dispose of an asset of the estate, including real property in another state, for cash or on credit, at public or private sale, and manage, develop, improve, exchange, partition, change the character of, or abandon an asset of the estate;

(h) Make ordinary or extraordinary repairs or alterations in buildings or other structures, demolish any improvements, and raze existing or erect new party walls or buildings;

(i) Subdivide, develop, or dedicate land to public use, make or obtain the vacation of plats and adjust boundaries, adjust differences in valuation or exchange or partition by giving or receiving considerations, and dedicate easements to public use without consideration;

(j) Enter for any purpose into a lease as lessor or lessee, with or without option to purchase or renew, for a term within or extending beyond the term of the conservatorship;

(k) Enter into a lease or arrangement for exploration and removal of minerals or other natural resources or enter into a pooling or unitization agreement;

(l) Grant an option involving disposition of an asset of the estate and take an option for the acquisition of any asset;

(m) Vote a security, in person or by general or limited proxy;

(n) Pay calls, assessments, and any other sums chargeable or accruing against or on account of securities;

(o) Sell or exercise stock subscription or conversion rights;

(p) Consent, directly or through a committee or other agent, to the reorganization, consolidation, merger, dissolution, or liquidation of a corporation or other business enterprise;

(q) Hold a security in the name of a nominee or in other form without disclosure of the conservatorship so that title to the security may pass by delivery;

(r) Insure the assets of the estate against damage or loss and the conservator against liability with respect to a third person;

(s) Borrow money, with or without security, to be repaid from the estate or otherwise and advance money for the protection of the estate or the protected person and for all expenses, losses, and liability sustained in the administration of the estate or because of the holding or ownership of any assets, for which the conservator has a lien on the estate as against the protected person for advances so made;

(t) Pay or contest any claim, settle a claim by or against the estate or the protected person by compromise, arbitration, or otherwise, and release, in whole or in part, any claim belonging to the estate to the extent the claim is uncollectible;

(u) Pay taxes, assessments, compensation of the conservator and any guardian, and other expenses incurred in the collection, care, administration, and protection of the estate;

(v) Allocate items of income or expense to income or principal of the estate, as provided by other law, including creation of reserves out of income for depreciation, obsolescence, or amortization or for depletion of minerals or other natural resources;

(w) Pay any sum distributable to a protected person or individual who is in fact dependent on the protected person by paying the sum to the distributee or by paying the sum for the use of the distributee:

> (I) To the guardian of the distributee;
>
> (II) To a distributee's custodian under the "Colorado Uniform Transfers to Minors Act", article 50 of title 11, C.R.S., or custodial trustee under the "Colorado Uniform Custodial Trust Act", article 1.5 of this title; or
>
> (III) If there is no guardian, custodian, or custodial trustee, to a relative or other person having physical custody of the distributee;

(x) Prosecute or defend actions, claims, or proceedings in any jurisdiction for the protection of assets of the estate and of the conservator in the performance of fiduciary duties; and

(y) Execute and deliver all instruments that will accomplish or facilitate the exercise of the powers vested in the conservator.

(3) Except as otherwise qualified or limited by the court in its order of appointment and endorsed on the letters, a conservator may exercise any of the powers enumerated in the "Colorado Fiduciaries' Powers Act", part 8 of article 1 of this title.

(4) The court may confer on a conservator at the time of appointment or later, in addition to the powers conferred by sections 15-14-425, 15-14-426, and 15-14-427, any power that the court itself could exercise under section 15-14-410. The court may, at the time of appointment or later, limit the powers of a conservator otherwise conferred by sections 15-14-425, 15-14-426, and 15-14-427, or previously conferred by the court, and may at any time relieve the conservator of any limitation. If the court limits any power conferred on the conservator by section 15-14-425, 15-14-426, or 15-14-427 or specifies, as provided in section 15-14-421 (1) that title to some but not all assets of the protected person vest in the conservator, the limitation shall be endorsed upon the conservator's letters of appointment.

(5) In investing the estate, and in selecting assets of the estate for distribution under section 15-14-427, in utilizing powers of revocation or withdrawal available for the support of the protected person and exercisable by the conservator or the court, and in exercising any other powers vested in them, the conservator and the court should take into account any known estate plan of the protected person, including his or her will, any

revocable trust of which he or she is settlor, and any contract, transfer, or joint ownership arrangement with provisions for payment or transfer of benefits or interests at his or her death to another or others which he or she may have originated. The conservator may examine the will of the protected person.

15-14-425.5. Authority to petition for dissolution of marriage or legal separation.

(1) The conservator may petition the court for authority to commence and maintain an action for dissolution of marriage or legal separation on behalf of the protected person. The court may grant such authority only if satisfied, after notice and hearing, that:
> (a) It is in the best interests of the protected person based on evidence of abandonment, abuse, exploitation, or other compelling circumstances, and the protected person either is incapable of consenting; or
> (b) The protected person has consented to the proposed dissolution of marriage or legal separation.

(2) Nothing in this section shall be construed as modifying the statutory grounds for dissolution of marriage and legal separation as set forth in section 14-10-106, C.R.S.

15-14-426. Delegation.

(1) A conservator may not delegate to an agent or another conservator the entire administration of the estate, but a conservator may otherwise delegate the performance of functions that a prudent trustee of comparable skills may delegate under similar circumstances.

(2) The conservator shall exercise reasonable care, skill, and caution in:
> (a) Selecting an agent;
> (b) Establishing the scope and terms of a delegation, consistent with the purposes and terms of the conservatorship;
> (c) Periodically reviewing an agent's overall performance and compliance with the terms of the delegation; and
> (d) Redressing an action or decision of an agent that would constitute a breach of trust if performed by the conservator.

(3) A conservator who complies with subsections (1) and (2) of this section is not liable to the protected person or to the estate or to the protected person's successors for the decisions or actions of the agent to whom a function was delegated.

(4) In performing a delegated function, an agent shall exercise reasonable care to comply with the terms of the delegation.

(5) By accepting a delegation from a conservator subject to the laws of this state, an agent submits to the jurisdiction of the courts of this state.

15-14-427. Principles of distribution by conservator.

(1) Unless otherwise specified in the order of appointment and endorsed on the letters of appointment or contrary to the financial plan filed pursuant to section 15-14-418, a conservator may expend or distribute income or principal of the estate of the protected person without further court authorization or confirmation for the support, care, education, health, and welfare of the protected person and individuals who are in fact dependent on the protected person, including the payment of child support or spousal maintenance, in accordance with the following rules:

(a) A conservator shall consider recommendations relating to the appropriate standard of support, care, education, health, and welfare for the protected person or an individual who is in fact dependent on the protected person made by a guardian, if any, and, if the protected person is a minor, the conservator shall consider recommendations made by a parent.

(b) A conservator may not be surcharged for money paid to persons furnishing support, care, education, or benefit to a protected person, or an individual who is in fact dependent on the protected person, in accordance with the recommendations of a parent or guardian of the protected person unless the conservator knows that the parent or guardian derives personal financial benefit therefrom, including relief from any personal duty of support, or the recommendations are not in the best interest of the protected person.

(c) In making distributions under this paragraph (c), the conservator shall consider:

(I) The size of the estate, the estimated duration of the conservatorship, and the likelihood that the protected person, at some future time, may be fully self-sufficient and able to manage his or her business affairs and the estate;

(II) The accustomed standard of living of the protected person and individuals who are in fact dependent on the protected person; and

(III) Other money or sources used for the support of the protected person.

(d) Money expended under this paragraph (d) may be paid by the conservator to any person, including the protected person, as reimbursement for expenditures that the conservator might have made, or in advance for services to be rendered to the protected person if it is reasonable to expect the services will be performed and advance payments are customary or reasonably necessary under the circumstances.

(2) If an estate is ample to provide for the distributions authorized by subsection (1) of this section, a conservator for a protected person other than a minor may make gifts that the protected person might have been expected to make, in amounts that do not exceed in the aggregate for any calendar year twenty percent of the income of the estate in that year.

15-14-428. Death of protected person.

(1) If a protected person dies, the conservator shall deliver to the court for safekeeping any will of the protected person that is in the conservator's possession or control, inform

the personal representative or devisees named in the will of the delivery, and retain the estate for delivery to the personal representative of the decedent or to another person entitled to it.

(2) After the death of the protected person, the conservator shall make no expenditures of conservatorship funds except with court authorization other than necessary to preserve the assets of the estate. However, the conservator may release funds for the funeral, cremation, or burial of the deceased protected person if necessary to do so under the circumstances.

15-14-429. Presentation and allowance of claims.

(1) A conservator may pay, or secure by encumbering assets of the estate, claims against the estate or against the protected person arising before or during the conservatorship upon their presentation and allowance in accordance with the priorities stated in subsection (4) of this section. A claimant may present a claim by:
>(a) Sending or delivering to the conservator a written statement of the claim, indicating its basis, the name and address of the claimant, and the amount claimed; or
>>(b) Filing a written statement of the claim, in a form prescribed by rule, with the clerk of the court and sending or delivering a copy of the statement to the conservator.

(2) A claim is deemed presented on receipt of the written statement of claim by the conservator or the filing of the claim with the court, whichever first occurs. A presented claim is allowed if it is not disallowed by written statement sent or delivered by the conservator to the claimant within sixty days after its presentation. The conservator before payment may change an allowance to a disallowance in whole or in part, but not after allowance under a court order or judgment or an order directing payment of the claim. The presentation of a claim tolls the running of any statute of limitations relating to the claim until thirty days after its disallowance. If a claim is not yet due, the date when it will become due shall be stated. If a claim is contingent or unliquidated, the nature of the uncertainty or the anticipated due date of the claim shall be stated.

(3) A claimant whose claim has not been paid may petition the court for determination of the claim at any time before it is barred by a statute of limitations and, upon due proof, procure an order for its allowance, payment, or security by encumbering assets of the estate. If a proceeding is pending against a protected person at the time of appointment of a conservator or is initiated against the protected person thereafter, the moving party shall give to the conservator notice of any proceeding that could result in creating a claim against the estate.

(4) If it appears that the estate is likely to be exhausted before all existing claims are paid, the conservator shall distribute the estate in money or in kind in payment of claims in the following order:
>(a) Costs and expenses of administration;

(b) Claims of the federal or state government having priority under other law;

(c) Claims incurred by the conservator for support, care, education, health, and welfare previously provided to the protected person or individuals who are in fact dependent on the protected person;

(d) Claims arising before the conservatorship; and

(e) All other claims.

(5) Allowed claims within the same class shall be paid pro rata. Preference may not be given in the payment of a claim over any other claim of the same class, and a claim due and payable may not be preferred over a claim not due.

(6) If assets of the conservatorship are adequate to meet all existing claims, the court, acting in the best interest of the protected person, may order the conservator to grant a security interest in the conservatorship estate for the payment of any or all claims at a future date.

(7) Nothing in this section affects or prevents:

(a) Any proceeding to enforce any mortgage, pledge, or other lien upon property of the estate; or

(b) To the limits of the insurance protection only, any proceeding to establish liability of the protected person for which he or she is protected by liability insurance.

(8) Unless otherwise provided in any judgment in another court entered against the protected person or the protected person's estate, an allowed claim bears interest at the legal rate for the period commencing sixty days after the time the claim was originally filed with the court or delivered to the conservator, unless based on a contract making a provision for interest, in which case, such claim bears interest in accordance with that contract's provisions.

15-14-430. Personal liability of conservator.

(1) Except as otherwise provided in the contract, a conservator is not personally liable on a contract properly entered into in a fiduciary capacity in the course of administration of the estate unless the conservator fails to reveal in the contract the representative capacity and identify the estate.

(2) A conservator is personally liable for obligations arising from ownership or control of property of the estate or for other acts or omissions occurring in the course of administration of the estate only if personally at fault.

(3) Claims based on contracts entered into by a conservator in a fiduciary capacity, obligations arising from ownership or control of the estate, and claims based on torts committed in the course of administration of the estate may be asserted against the estate by proceeding against the conservator in a fiduciary capacity, whether or not the conservator is personally liable therefore.

(4) A question of liability between the estate and the conservator personally may be determined in a proceeding for accounting, surcharge, or indemnification, or in another appropriate proceeding or action.

(5) A conservator is not personally liable for any environmental condition on or injury resulting from any environmental condition on land solely by reason of an acquisition of title under section 15-14-421.

15-14-431. Termination of proceedings.

(1) A conservatorship terminates upon the death of the protected person or upon order of the court determining that a conservatorship is no longer necessary or needed to protect the assets of the protected person. Unless created for reasons other than that the protected person is a minor, a conservatorship created for a minor also terminates when the protected person attains the age of twenty-one years. Upon learning of the protected person's death, the conservator shall promptly give notice of death to the court and all other persons designated to receive notice of subsequent actions in the order appointing the conservator.

(2) Upon receiving an order terminating the conservatorship or upon receiving notice of the death of a protected person, the conservator shall conclude the administration of the estate by filing a final report and a petition for discharge within sixty days after distribution unless otherwise directed by the court.

(3) On petition of a protected person, a conservator, or another person interested in a protected person's welfare, the court may terminate the conservatorship if the protected person no longer meets the statutory requirements for the creation of a conservatorship. Termination of the conservatorship without a decree of discharge does not affect a conservator's liability for previous acts or the obligation to account for funds and assets of the protected person.

(4) Except as otherwise ordered by the court for good cause, before terminating a conservatorship, the court shall follow the same procedures to safeguard the rights of the protected person that apply to a petition for conservatorship. The court shall order termination unless it is proved by clear and convincing evidence that continuation of the conservatorship is still statutorily warranted and is still in the best interest of the protected person.

(5) Upon termination of a conservatorship and whether or not formally distributed by the conservator, title to assets of the estate passes to the formerly protected person, the former protected person's successors, or as ordered by the court. The order of termination must provide for the payment of all fees, costs, and expenses of administration and direct the conservator to file appropriate instruments to evidence the transfer of title or confirm the ordered distribution pursuant to the schedule of distribution prior to receiving the decree of discharge.

(6) The court shall enter a decree of discharge upon being fully satisfied that the conservator has met all conditions required by the court for the conservator's discharge.

15-14-432. Payment of debt and delivery of property to foreign conservator without local proceeding.

(1) A person who is indebted to or has the possession of tangible or intangible property of a protected person may pay the debt or deliver the property to a foreign conservator, guardian of the estate, or other court-appointed fiduciary of the state of residence of the protected person. Payment or delivery may be made only upon proof of appointment and presentation of an affidavit made by or on behalf of the fiduciary stating that a protective proceeding relating to the protected person is not pending in this state and the foreign fiduciary is entitled to payment or to receive delivery.

(2) Payment or delivery in accordance with subsection (1) of this section discharges the debtor or possessor, absent knowledge of any protective proceeding pending in this state.

15-14-433. Foreign conservator - proof of authority - bond - powers.

If a conservator has not been appointed in this state and a petition in a protective proceeding is not pending in this state, a conservator appointed in the state in which the protected person resides may file in a district or probate court of this state, in a county in which property belonging to the protected person is located, authenticated copies of letters of appointment and of any bond. Thereafter, the conservator may exercise all powers of a conservator appointed in this state as to property in this state and may maintain actions and proceedings in this state subject to any conditions otherwise imposed upon nonresident parties.

Power of Attorney

This section of the manual defines and describes key terms used when referring to powers of attorney (POA), the various types of powers of attorney, the procedures involved in designating authority of an agent under a power of attorney, the duties of the agent under various types of powers of attorney, how the principal can change and revoke powers of attorney, and situations by which a power of attorney document becomes null and void. Responding to allegations of abuse by an agent having authority under a power of attorney is addressed in the final section of the manual.

The terms used in reference to powers of attorney include:

➢ **"Principal"** refers to the person giving power of attorney to another.
➢ **"Agent"** refers to the person appointed by the principal to assume the duties specified under a power of attorney.
➢ **"Agency"** refers to the relationship between the principal and the agent.
➢ **"Agency instrument"** refers to the written power of attorney document.
➢ **"Third party"** refers to a person or company requested by the agent to deal with a principal's property as authorized in the agency instrument.

Types of Powers of Attorney

A power of attorney is a document that gives an agent the authority to act on the behalf of a principal. There are several types of powers of attorney:

- Power of Attorney (POA)
- Limited Power of Attorney (POA)
- Durable Power of Attorney (DPOA)
- Medical Durable Power of Attorney (MDPOA)
- Springing Power of Attorney (POA)

A **power of attorney (POA)** grants the agent broad authority *only* over the principal's finances. The POA allows the agent to act on behalf of the principal in a wide range of financial transactions, only as specified in the POA document. A POA expires if the principal loses decisional capacity, unless the agency instrument states otherwise.

A **limited power of attorney (POA),** grants the agent specific rights, such as check-writing authority, for a limited time (for example, while the principal is on an extended vacation). A limited power of attorney expires if the principal loses decisional capacity, unless the agency instrument states otherwise.

A **durable power of attorney (DPOA)** grants the agent broad financial (not medical) authority. The term "durable" refers to the fact that this form of POA *remains in effect* should the principal lose decisional capacity. To be durable, the document must contain wording such as "this power of attorney shall not be affected by the subsequent incapacity or disability of the principal." The agent's authority is subject to any directive, condition, or limitation set forth by the principal in the DPOA document.

A **medical durable power of attorney (MDPOA),** grants the agent authority to make medical treatment decisions on behalf of the principal should the principal lose decisional capacity. Such medical treatment also includes artificial nourishment and hydration. The term "durable" refers to the fact that this form of POA *remains in effect* should the principal lose decisional capacity. The principal may specify in the medical durable power of attorney agency instrument any directive, condition, or limitation of the agent's authority. Detailed information about MDPOA can be found in the Medical Advance Directives section of this manual.

A **springing power of attorney** grants the agent authority to make decisions on behalf of the principal at a specified time or event in the future. The most common event that marks the beginning of authority for an agent under a springing POA is when the principal loses decisional capacity. A springing POA allows the principal to provide his/her own criteria for the determination or substantiation of "incapacity." Often, the springing POA agency instrument will stipulate the triggering event, such as a medical condition, for the agent to assume responsibility. The springing power of attorney remains in effect until the principal's death, until revoked by a court, or until the event or disability ends.

Procedure for Obtaining Powers Of Attorney

1) The principal, or an attorney on behalf of the principal, may develop the written power of attorney document.

2) The principal determines the scope of the agent's authority including all power of attorney designations.

3) Forms for financial powers of attorney designations (including durable powers of attorney) are available within the statutes at C.R.S. 15-14-610(2), attorneys' offices, through the Guardianship Alliance of Colorado, and in some office supply stores. Forms may also be found at Bradford Forms Publishing on the Internet at www.bradfordpublishing.com under "Personal Property and Miscellaneous Forms."

4) Notarization and witnessing of the signing of financial power of attorney documents is highly recommended and is required in real estate transactions in Colorado.

5) If questions arise regarding the specific authority given to an agent, it is advisable to consult with the local county attorney, or other objective attorney, and request a review of the agency instrument.

6) *Please note that all forms of POA's may be referred to merely as a "POA." It is essential that the actual POA document (agency instrument) be reviewed to clarify the extent and type of authority given to the agent in each case.*

Duties and Powers of Agents Under a Financial Power Of Attorney

Each document authorizing a power of attorney is unique to the principal. An overview of typical duties and powers of the agent are provided below.

1) The agent should **act in the best interests of the principal**.

2) The agent may **exercise a number of powers on behalf of the principal** as noted in the POA document. These powers may pertain to the following areas:

   a. Real Estate Matters: The agent may buy, sell, rent, and manage property, take out mortgages, and execute deeds.

   b. Personal Property Matters: The agent may buy, sell, and manage all types of goods such as vehicles, furniture, jewelry, and other types of personal property.

   c. Banking Transactions: The agent may sign checks, withdraw funds, open accounts, borrow money, and remove items from the principal's safe deposit box.

   d. Stock and Bond Transactions: The agent may buy, sell, and exchange stocks, bonds, and mutual funds, and vote as a shareholder.

   e. Business Operating Transactions: The agent may manage, operate and sell any businesses the principal owns, including partnerships and closely held corporations; buy or expand businesses; and exercise rights as a business partner or bond holder.

   f. Retirement Plans: The agent may manage retirement and pension plans, including exercising investment powers, designating beneficiaries, making contributions, and borrowing against or selling assets.

   g. Insurance and Annuities: The agent may take out insurance policies for the principal or the principal's family, modify them, borrow against them, and surrender them for their present cash value.

   h. Estate and Trust Matters: The agent may act in all matters pertaining to a trust, estate or other fund from which the principal is entitled, and has the power to transfer property to the principal's living trust.

   i. Legal Matters: The agent may hire attorneys for the principal, act for the principal in legal matters, sign legal documents, and sue on behalf of the principal.

   j. Government Assistance: The agent may collect Social Security, Medicare, Medicaid, and any other government benefits.

   k. Taxes: The agent may file and sign tax returns, represent the principal in all tax matters, and receive confidential information and refund checks.

   l. Personal and Family Care: The agent may take care of the principal's spouse and children and maintain their accustomed standard of living, including paying for health care, education, food, and housing.

m. Making Gifts: The agent may make gifts to others from the principal's property and assets, although the principal maintains the option of restricting the agent from making gifts to the agent.

3) The agent is **liable for any breach of legal duty** owed the principal.

4) The agent is **required to observe a standard in dealing with the assets** of the principal that would be observed by a prudent person dealing with the property of another.

5) The agent is **required to keep records** of receipts, disbursements, and significant actions taken on behalf of the principal.

6) The agent is **required to give the principal a full accounting of activity** if requested by the principal. The agent is not legally required to file reports with anyone else, unless so stated in the agency instrument.

7) The **agent's role when the principal has a court appointed guardian and/or conservator** consists of the following:

   a. The agent must consult with one or both regarding the financial affairs of the principal.
   b. The agent maintains the durable POA given to him/her by the principal, unless the court order resulting from a guardianship appointment states otherwise.

8) **Specific powers, limitations, and liabilities of the agent and the guardian and/or conservator** when the principal has both a POA and a court appointed guardian and/or conservator are:

   a. A guardian has the same authority as the principal to revoke, suspend, or terminate the agency relating to non-health care decisions, subject to limitations specified in guardianship orders.
   b. A guardian cannot revoke a medical durable power of attorney without a court order.
   c. An agent's healthcare decision under a MDPOA takes precedence over that of a guardian unless otherwise ordered by the court.
   d. A guardian has recourse through the court to remove an agent who becomes incapacitated, who refuses to serve, or whose action or inaction causes or threatens substantial harm to the principal.
   e. A conservator has the same authority as the principal to continue, modify, or revoke the protected person's financial power of attorney without a court order.
   f. A conservator may require the agent to provide an accounting of the protected person's finances.

g. A noncompliant agent will be liable for all costs incurred in obtaining compliance, including, but not limited to, conservator and attorney fees.

Changing or Revoking Powers of Attorney

All powers of attorney (POA) may be revoked or changed at any time by the principal. Even a principal who has lost decisional capacity has the right to change or revoke the POA. The original agency instrument and all copies that were distributed should be destroyed and replaced with the new or revised agency instrument, if applicable.

1) The principal may choose to change or revoke a POA designation if:

   a. The principal believes that the existing agent is no longer making decisions in the best interest of the principal.
   b. The principal decides that it is no longer necessary to have an agent because the POA was designated due to a special event or circumstance.
   c. The principal's spouse serves as agent, and the couple divorces or is granted a legal separation.

2) The principal dies, the agent's authority under the agency instrument terminates.

Statutes Relating to Power of Attorney

The statutes included in this manual are listed below:

Title 15, Article 14, Part 6 Power Of Attorney

15-14-601. Legislative declaration.

(1) The general assembly hereby recognizes that each adult individual has the right as a principal to appoint an agent to deal with property or make personal decisions for the individual, but that this right cannot be fully effective unless the principal may empower the agent to act throughout the principal's lifetime, including during periods of disability, and be sure that any third party will honor the agent's authority at all times.

(2) The general assembly hereby finds, determines, and declares that:
(a) In light of modern financial needs, the statutory recognition of the right of and the permissible scope of the agent's authority, to clarify the power of the individual to authorize an agent to make financial decisions for the individual, and to better protect any third party who relies in good faith on the agent so that reliance will be assured.
(b) The public interest requires a standard form affidavit of agency that any third party may use to assure that an agent's authority under an agency has not been altered or terminated.

(3) The general assembly hereby finds, determines, and declares that nothing in this part 6 shall be deemed to authorize or encourage any course of action that violates the criminal laws of this state or the United States. Similarly, nothing in this part 6 shall be deemed to authorize or encourage any violation of any civil right expressed in the constitution, statutes, case law, or administrative rulings of this state or the United States or any course of action that violates the public policy expressed in the

constitution, statutes, case law, or administrative rulings of this state or the United States.

(4) The general assembly hereby recognizes each adult's constitutional right to accept or reject medical treatment, artificial nourishment, and hydration and the right to create advanced medical directives and to appoint an agent to make health care decisions under a medical durable power of attorney. The "Colorado Patient Autonomy Act", sections 15-14-503 to 15-14-509, is intended to assist the exercise of such rights.

(5) In the event of a conflict between the provisions of this part 6 and the "Colorado Patient Autonomy Act" or between the provisions of powers of attorney prepared pursuant to this part 6 and the "Colorado Patient Autonomy Act", the provisions of the "Colorado Patient Autonomy Act" or provisions of powers of attorney prepared pursuant to the "Colorado Patient Autonomy Act" shall prevail.

(6) This part 6 does not abridge the right of any person to enter into a verbal principal and agent relationship. A brokerage relationship between a real estate broker and a seller, landlord, buyer, or tenant in a real estate transaction established pursuant to part 8 of article 61 of title 12, C.R.S., shall be governed by the provisions of part 8 of article 61 of title 12, C.R.S., and not by this part 6.

(7) This part 6 does not create any power or right in an agent that the agent's principal does not hold or possess and does not abridge contracts existing between principals and third parties.

15-14-602. Definitions.

As used in this part 6:

(1) "Agency" means the relationship between the principal and the principal's agent.

(2) "Agency instrument" means the written power of attorney or other written instrument of agency governing the relationship between the principal and agent. An agency is subject to the provisions of this part 6 to the extent the agency relationship is established in writing and may be controlled by the principal, excluding agencies and powers for the benefit of the agent. This definition shall not apply to medical powers of attorney drafted pursuant to the "Colorado Patient Autonomy Act", sections 15-14-503 to 15-14-509.

(3) "Agent" means the attorney-in-fact or other person, including successors, who is authorized by the agency instrument to act for the principal.

(4) "Principal" means an individual, corporation, trust, partnership, limited liability company, or other entity, including, but not limited to, an individual acting as trustee, personal representative, or other fiduciary, who signs a power of attorney or other instrument of agency granting powers to an agent.

(5) "Third party" means any person who is requested by an agent under an agency instrument to recognize the agent's authority to deal with the principal's property or who acts in good-faith reliance on a copy of the agency instrument. "Third party" includes an individual, corporation, trust, partnership, limited liability company, or other entity, as may be appropriate.

15-14-603. Applicability.

(1)   (a) The principal may specify in the agency instrument:
        (I) The event upon which or time when the agency begins and terminates;
        (II) The mode of revocation or amendment of the agency instrument; and
        (III) The rights, powers, duties, limitations, immunities, and other terms applicable to the agent and to all third parties dealing with the agent.
    (b) The provisions of the agency instrument control in the case of a conflict between the provisions of the agency instrument and the provisions of this part 6. In the agency instrument, the principal may authorize the agent to appoint a successor agent.

(2)   (a) Except as otherwise provided in this part 6, on or after January 1, 1995:
        (I) The provisions of this part 6 govern every agency instrument, whenever and wherever executed, and all acts of the agent, to the extent the provisions of this part 6 are not inconsistent with the agency instrument; and
        (II) The provisions of this part 6 apply to all agency instruments exercised in Colorado and to all other agency instruments if the principal is a resident of Colorado at the time the agency instrument is signed or at the time of exercise or if the agency instrument indicates that Colorado law is to apply.
    (b) The statutory power of attorney for property form set forth in section 15-1-1302 does not limit the applicability of the provisions of this part 6. It is the general assembly's intent that every agency instrument, including but not limited to statutory agency instruments, shall have the benefit of and be governed by all of the general provisions of this part 6, except as otherwise provided in this part 6 or to the extent the terms of the agency instrument are inconsistent with the provisions of this part 6.

(3)   (a) The authority of an attorney-in-fact or an agent to act on behalf of the principal may include, but is not limited to, the powers specified in sections 15-14-501 to 15-14-506.
    (b) Any durable power of attorney executed under this part 6 may also have a document with a written statement as provided in section 12-34-105 (1) (c), C.R.S., or a statement in substantially similar form, indicating a decision regarding organ and tissue donation. Such a document shall be executed in accordance with the provisions of the "Uniform Anatomical Gift Act", article 34 of title 12, C.R.S. Such a written statement may be in the following form:

I hereby make an anatomical gift, to be effective upon my death, of:
A.____ Any needed organs/tissues
B.____ The following organs/tissues:

_____

Donor signature: _____

(4) A principal must be at least eighteen years of age to execute an agency instrument under the provisions of this part 6. A natural person must be at least twenty-one years of age to be appointed as an agent under an agency instrument.

15-14-604. Duration of agency - amendment and revocation - effect of disability - resignation of agent.

(1) Where an agency instrument contains the language specified in section 15-14-501 (1) or otherwise specifies that the agent designated therein may exercise the authority conferred notwithstanding the principal's disability, such agent may exercise such authority notwithstanding the principal's later disability or incapacity or later uncertainty as to whether the principal is dead.

(2) Any agency created by an agency instrument continues until the death of the principal, regardless of the length of time that elapses, unless the agency instrument states an earlier termination date. The principal may amend or revoke the agency instrument at any time and in any manner that is communicated to the agent or to any other person who is related to the subject matter of the agency. Any agent who acts in good faith on behalf of the principal within the scope of an agency instrument is not liable for any acts that are no longer authorized by reason of an amendment or revocation of the agency instrument until the agent receives actual notice of the amendment or revocation. An agency may be temporarily continued under the conditions specified in section 15-14-607.

(3) All acts of the agent that are within the scope of the agency and are committed during any period of disability, incapacity, or incompetency of the principal have the same effect and inure to the benefit of and bind the principal and his or her successors in interest as if the principal were competent and not disabled.

(4) Any agent acting on behalf of a principal under an agency instrument has the right to resign under the terms and conditions stated in the agency instrument. If the agency instrument does not specify the terms and conditions of resignation, an agent may resign by notifying the principal, or the principal's guardian or conservator if one has been appointed, in writing of the agent's resignation. The agent shall also notify in writing the successor agent, if any, and all reasonably ascertainable third parties who are affected by the resignation. In all cases, any party who receives notice of the resignation of an agent is bound by such notice.

15-14-605. Dissolution of marriage.

If an agency instrument appoints the principal's spouse as agent and a court enters a decree of dissolution of marriage or legal separation between the principal and spouse after the agency instrument is signed, the spouse shall be deemed to have died at the time of the decree for purposes of the agency.

15-14-606. Duty - standard of care - record-keeping - exoneration.

Unless otherwise agreed by the principal and agent in the agency instrument, an agent is under no duty to exercise the powers granted by the agency or to assume control of or responsibility for any of the principal's property, care, or affairs, regardless of the principal's physical or mental condition. Whenever the agent exercises the powers granted by the agency, the agent shall use due care to act in the best interests of the principal in accordance with the terms of the agency. Any agent who acts under an agency instrument shall be liable for any breach of legal duty owed by the agent to the principal under Colorado law. The agent shall keep a record of all receipts, disbursements, and significant actions taken under the agency. The agent shall not be liable for any loss due to the act or default of any other person. When exercising any powers under an agency during any period of disability of the principal, the agent shall be held to the standard of care of a fiduciary as specified in sections 15-16-302 and 15-14-418.

15-14-607. Reliance on an agency instrument.

(1)   (a) Any third party who acts in good-faith reliance on an agency instrument that is duly notarized shall be fully protected and released to the same extent as if such third party dealt directly with the principal as a fully competent person. Upon demand of any third party, the agent shall furnish an affidavit that states that the agency instrument relied upon is a true copy of the agency instrument and that, to the best of the agent's knowledge, the principal is alive and the relevant powers of the agent have not been altered or terminated; however, any third party who acts in good-faith reliance on an agency instrument shall be protected regardless of whether such third party demands or receives an affidavit.

(b)   (I) Any third party who deals with an agent may presume, in the absence of actual knowledge to the contrary, that:

(A) The agency instrument naming the agent was validly executed;
(B) The principal was competent at the time of execution; and
(C) At the time of reliance, the principal is alive, the agency instrument and the relevant powers of the agent have not terminated or been amended, and the acts of the agent conform to the standards of this part 6.

(II) Any third party who relies on an agency instrument shall not be responsible for the proper application of any property delivered to or controlled by the agent or for questioning the authority of the agent.

(2) Any person to whom the agent, operating under a duly notarized agency instrument, communicates a direction that is in accordance with the terms of the agency instrument shall comply with such direction. Any person who arbitrarily or without reasonable cause fails to comply with such direction shall be subject to the costs, expenses, and reasonable attorney fees required to appoint a conservator for the principal, to obtain a declaratory judgment, or to obtain an order pursuant to section 15-14-412. This subsection (2) shall not apply to the sale, transfer, encumbrance, or conveyance of real property.

(3) Any third party that has reasonable cause to question the authenticity, validity, or authority of an agency instrument or agency may make prompt and reasonable inquiry of the agent, the principal, or other persons involved for additional information and may submit an interpleader action to the district court or the probate court of the county in which the principal resides by depositing any funds or other assets that may be affected by the agency instrument with the appropriate court. In such an interpleader action, if the court finds that the third party had reasonable cause to commence the action, the third party shall be entitled to all reasonable expenses and costs incurred by the third party in bringing the interpleader action.

(4) Any third party may require an agent to present, as proof of the agency, either the original agency instrument naming such agent or a facsimile thereof certified by a notary. The third party has discretion to determine whether the agent shall provide the original agency instrument or a certified facsimile.

15-14-608. Preservation of estate plan and trusts.

(1) In exercising any powers granted under the agency instrument, the agent shall take the principal's estate plan into account, insofar as it is known to the agent, and shall attempt to preserve the estate plan. Specifically, the agent shall preserve the estate plan in exercising any powers of amendment or revocation and any powers to expend or withdraw property passing by trust, contract, or beneficiary designation at the principal's death, including, but not limited to, specifically bequeathed property, joint accounts, life insurance, trusts, and retirement plans. The agent shall be liable to a beneficiary only for actions taken in bad faith.

(2) An agent may not revoke or amend a trust that is revocable or amendable by the principal without specific authority and specific reference to the trust in the agency instrument. In addition, an agent may not require the trustee of any trust for the benefit of the principal to pay income or principal to the agent without specific authority and specific reference to the trust in the agency instrument. The agent shall have access to and the right to copy, but not to hold, the principal's will, trusts, and other personal

papers and records to the extent the agent deems necessary for purposes of exercising the agency powers.

15-14-609. Agency - court relationship.

(1) Upon petition by any interested person, including the agent, after such notice to interested persons as the court directs and upon a finding by the court that the principal lacks the capacity to control or revoke the agency instrument:

(a) If the court finds that the agent is not acting for the benefit of the principal in accordance with the terms of the agency instrument or that the agent's action or inaction has caused or threatens substantial harm to the principal's person or property in a manner not authorized or intended by the principal, the court may order a guardian of the principal's person or a conservator of the principal's estate, or both, to exercise any powers of the principal under the agency instrument, including the power to revoke the agency, or may enter such other orders without appointment of a guardian or conservator as the court deems necessary to provide for the best interests of the principal; or

(b) If the court finds that the agency instrument requires interpretation, the court may construe the agency instrument and instruct the agent to act in accordance with its construction; except that the court may not amend the agency instrument. A court may order a guardian or conservator, or both, to exercise powers of the principal under the agency instrument.

(2) Proceedings under this section shall be commenced in the court where the guardian or conservator was appointed. If no Colorado guardian or conservator has been appointed, proceedings shall be commenced in the county where the principal resides. If the principal does not reside in Colorado, proceedings may be commenced in any county in the state.

(3)   (a) If a guardian or conservator is appointed for the principal, the agent shall consult with the guardian or conservator during the continuance of the appointment on matters concerning the principal's financial affairs.

(b) A conservator has the same power to revoke, suspend, or terminate all or any part of the power of attorney or agency instrument as it relates to financial matters as the principal would have had if the principal were not disabled or incompetent.

(c) Subject to any limitation or restriction included in the letters of guardianship, a guardian has the same power to revoke, suspend, or terminate all or any part of the power of attorney or agency instrument as it relates to matters concerning the principal's personal care that the principal would have had if the principal were not disabled or incompetent, except with respect to medical treatment decisions made by an agent pursuant to sections 15-14-506 to 15-14-509. The exception included in this paragraph (c) shall not preclude a court from removing an agent in the event the agent becomes incapacitated or is unwilling or unable to serve as an agent.

15-14-610. Statutory form agent's affidavit regarding power of attorney.

(1) The form specified in subsection (2) of this section shall be known as the "statutory agent's affidavit regarding power of attorney" and may be used to assure that an agent's authority under an agency instrument has not been altered or terminated. An agent's affidavit in substantially the following form shall have the meaning and effect prescribed in this part 6. Nothing in this part 6 shall invalidate or bar the use of any other or different form of agent affidavit.

(2) The statutory agent's affidavit regarding power of attorney shall be in substantially the following form:

COLORADO AGENT'S AFFIDAVIT REGARDING POWER OF ATTORNEY
STATE OF COLORADO   )
) ss.
County of _____)
   I, _____, whose address is _____, of lawful age, pursuant to sections 15-1-1302, 15-14-501, and 15-14-502, Colorado Revised Statutes, state upon my oath that I am the attorney-in-fact and agent for _____, principal, under the power of attorney dated _____, a copy of which is attached hereto and incorporated herein by this reference, that as of this date I have no actual knowledge of the [revocation or*] termination of the power of attorney by any act of the principal, or by the death, [disability, or incompetence*] of the principal, that my authority has not been terminated by a decree of dissolution of marriage or legal separation, and that to the best of my knowledge the power of attorney has not been so terminated and remains valid, in full force and effect.
Dated: _____

_____
Attorney-in-Fact
The foregoing Affidavit was subscribed and sworn to before me on _____,
20___, by _____, Agent. Witness my hand and official seal. My Commission expires:

_____
        [SEAL]

Notary Public   _____

*Strike "revocation or" and "disability or incompetence" if the power of attorney is durable and the principal is disabled or incompetent.

15-14-611. Applicability of part.

This part 6 does not in any way invalidate any agency or power of attorney executed or any act of any agent, guardian, or conservator done or affect any claim, right, or remedy that accrued prior to January 1, 1995.

Medical Advance Directives

This section of the manual covers forms of medical decision-making and advance directives available for adults in Colorado. These include the CPR directive (also known as Directives Relating to Cardiopulmonary Resuscitation), living will (as established in the Colorado Medical Treatment Decision Act), medical durable power of attorney, and authority under the Proxy Decision-Makers for Medical Treatment statute. Each section gives basic information needed to create, implement, change, or revoke the advance directive.

Terms used in reference to advance medical directives include:

> "**Adult**" refers to any person eighteen years of age or older.
> "**Advance medical directive**" refers to any written instructions concerning the making of medical treatment decisions on behalf of the person who has provided the instructions. An advance medical directive includes a medical durable power of attorney, a living will, a power of attorney granting medical treatment authority, and/or a CPR directive, or designation of a proxy decision maker.
> "**Agent**" refers to the person appointed by the principal to assume the duties specified under a power of attorney.
> "**Agency**" refers to the relationship between the principal and the agent.
> "**Agency instrument**" refers to the written power of attorney document.
> "**Artificial nourishment and hydration**" means any medical procedure whereby nourishment or hydration is supplied through a tube inserted into a person's nose, mouth, stomach, or intestines, or when nutrients or fluids are injected intravenously into a person's bloodstream.
> "**Cardiopulmonary resuscitation**" or "**CPR**" refers to measures to restore cardiac function or to support breathing in the event of cardiac or respiratory arrest or malfunction. CPR includes, but is not limited to, chest compression, delivering electric shock to the chest, or placing tubes in the airway to assist breathing.
> "**Decisional capacity**" refers to the ability to provide informed consent to or refusal of medical treatment.
> "**Declarant**" refers to a mentally competent adult who signs a living will document.
> "**Declaration**" refers to a written document (living will) voluntarily signed in accordance with the requirements of section C.R.S. 15-18-104.
> "**Guardian ad litem**" (GAL) is a person appointed by the court to take legal action on behalf of the respondent. The guardian ad litem is charged with representing and making recommendations that are in the respondent's best interest. (For more detailed information on GAL, read C.R.S. 15-10-403 (5), C.R.S. 15-14-115 and Rule 15, Colorado Rules of Probate Procedure.)
> "**Life-sustaining procedure**" refers to any medical procedure or intervention that, if administered to a qualified patient, would serve only to prolong the dying

process. "Life-sustaining procedure" shall not include any medical procedure or intervention for nourishment of the qualified patient, or any medical procedure or intervention considered necessary by the attending physician to provide comfort or alleviate pain. However, artificial nourishment may be withdrawn or withheld pursuant to section C.R.S. 15-18-104 (2.5).

➢ **"Medical treatment"** refers to the provision, withholding, or withdrawal of any health care, medical procedure, including artificially provided nourishment and hydration, surgery, cardiopulmonary resuscitation, or service to maintain, diagnose, treat, or provide for a patient's physical or mental health or personal care.

➢ **"Qualified patient"** refers to a patient who has signed a living will declaration in accordance with the Colorado Medical Treatment Decision Act and who has been certified by the attending physician and one other physician to be in a terminal condition.

➢ **"Terminal condition"** refers to an incurable or irreversible condition for which the administration of life-sustaining procedures will serve only to postpone the moment of death.

➢ **"Third party"** refers to a person or company requested by the agent to deal with a principal's property as authorized in an agency instrument.

Types of Medical Advance Directives

The types of medical advance directives used in Colorado include:

- CPR Directive (cardiopulmonary resuscitation directive)
- Living Will (Colorado Medical Treatment Decision Act)
- Medical Durable Power of Attorney
- Proxy Decision Maker

A **"CPR directive"** is an advance medical directive pertaining to the administration of cardiopulmonary resuscitation.

A **living will** affirms the right of a competent adult to accept or reject medical or surgical treatment and creates a procedure by which a competent adult may make such decisions in advance, before the adult becomes unconscious or otherwise incompetent to make such a decision.

A **medical durable power of attorney** (MDPOA) allows any adult (principal) to grant another person (agent) authority to make medical treatment decisions on behalf of the principal should the principal lose decisional capacity.

A **proxy decision maker** for medical treatment makes decisions on behalf of an incapacitated adult, should that adult lack the decisional capacity to provide informed consent, refusal, or discontinuation of medical treatment. Family members and interested persons must come to a consensus and choose the proxy decision maker.

All advance directives may be signed by any person age 18 years or any person who is authorized to make medical decisions for another adult, such as a guardian, an agent under a medical durable power of attorney, or a proxy decision maker.

Prepared forms for advance medical directives are generic in nature. Whenever possible it is helpful to personalize the advance directive with the adult's own philosophy regarding "quality of life." For example, specific medical treatment preferences or objections regarding end of life decisions, such as, the use of a respirator, artificial nutrition, or pain medications, may be addressed.

CPR Directive

A **CPR (cardiopulmonary resuscitation) directive** informs medical personnel *not* to use CPR because the patient does not want it. Any adult over age eighteen who has the decisional capacity to provide informed consent to, or refusal of, medical treatment may sign a CPR directive. Any other person who is authorized to make medical treatment decisions on behalf of an incapacitated adult, such as a guardian, an agent under a medical durable power of attorney, or a proxy may sign a CPR directive for an individual who is already incapacitated.

Procedure for Creating a CPR Directive

1) A **CPR directive** can be written, in any form, by a competent adult or by the person who has medical decision-making authority for an incapacitated adult, such as a guardian, an agent under a medical durable power of attorney, or a proxy decision-maker for medical treatment. The directive is typically done on official state forms furnished by the Department of Public Health and Environment and available through most physicians' offices.

2) If a format other than the official state form is used as the directive, there is **standard required information** that must be included about the adult for whom the CPR directive is written:

   a. Name, sex, and date of birth
   b. Eye and hair color
   c. Race or ethnicity
   d. Name of hospice program, if applicable
   e. Attending physician's name, address, and phone number
   f. Directive concerning the administration of CPR

3) The **adult must sign the completed CPR directive** with his/her legal signature or mark. If the CPR directive was written by an adult's authorized decision maker, then the decision maker must sign the document. No witnesses are required to sign.

4) The directive concerning the administration of CPR must be dated and **countersigned by the attending physician**.

5) A **directive concerning organ and/or tissue donation** can also be written. A suggested form is located in the Resource section of this manual. However, any form is acceptable as long as it contains the information outlined above (2a-f). Statements within the directive should indicate that the adult wishes to make an

anatomical gift upon the adult's death and should specify which tissues are being donated.

6) The **directive concerning organ and/or tissue donation must be signed** by the adult or the adult's decision maker.

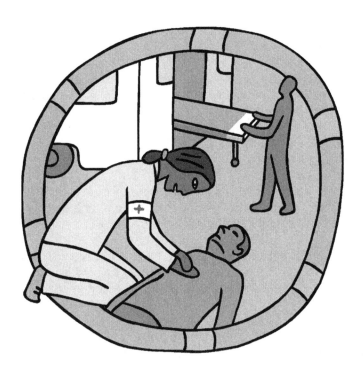

Implementation of a CPR Directive

The **CPR directive must be honored if it is apparent and immediately available to emergency medical service personnel, health care providers, and/or health care facilities**. Please note: Medical emergencies often result in a response from emergency medical personnel. A CPR directive will only be honored if it is present and available at the time of response.

1) Absence of a CPR directive presumes the adult consents to CPR measures.

2) No prosecution of any medical personnel or health care provider or facility will result from compliance with a CPR directive, as long as compliance was in good faith.

Revoking a CPR Directive

1) A CPR directive **may be revoked** at any time by the adult who is the subject of the directive. If a guardian, an agent under a medical durable power of attorney, or proxy originally signed the CPR directive on behalf of an incapacitated adult, then it may be revoked by that agent, guardian, or proxy if it is no longer medically indicated.

2) If the CPR directive was written by the adult at a time when the adult had decisional capacity, **it may not be revoked by a person who now has decision-making authority due to the adult's later incapacity.**

3) The CPR directive can be **revoked orally or by tearing up the original document.** It is important that anyone who had knowledge of the original CPR directive be informed of the decision to revoke the directive.

4) A decision to create a CPR directive is a critical decision. This decision should be **reviewed on a regular basis** by the adult or, if the adult's authorized decision-maker wrote the directive, by the decision maker.

Statutes Relating to a Cardiopulmonary Resuscitation Order

The statutes included in this manual are listed below:

Title 15, Article 18.6, Part 1 Directive Relating To Cardiopulmonary Resuscitation

15-18.6-101. Definitions.

As used in this article, unless the context otherwise requires:

(1) "Cardiopulmonary resuscitation" or "CPR" means measures to restore cardiac function or to support breathing in the event of cardiac or respiratory arrest or malfunction. "CPR" includes, but is not limited to, chest compression, delivering electric shock to the chest, or placing tubes in the airway to assist breathing.

(2) "CPR directive" means an advance medical directive pertaining to the administration of cardiopulmonary resuscitation.

(3) "Emergency medical service personnel" means any emergency medical technician at any level who is certified or licensed by the department of public health and environment. "Emergency medical service personnel" includes a first responder certified by the department of public health and environment or the division of fire safety in the office of preparedness, security, and fire safety in the department of public safety, in accordance with section 24-33.5-1205 (2) (c), C.R.S.

15-18.6-102. CPR directives for CPR - who may execute.

Any adult over age eighteen who has the decisional capacity to provide informed consent to or refusal of medical treatment or any other person who is, pursuant to the laws of this state or any other state, authorized to make medical treatment decisions on behalf of an adult who lacks such decisional capacity, may execute a CPR directive. After a physician issues a "do not resuscitate" order for a minor child, and only then, may the parents of the minor, if married and living together, the custodial parent or parent with decision-making responsibility for such a decision, or the legal guardian execute a CPR directive.

15-18.6-103. CPR directive forms - duties of state board of health.

(1) On or before January 1, 1993, the state board of health shall promulgate rules and protocols for the implementation of CPR directives by emergency medical service personnel. The protocols adopted by the board of health shall include uniform methods of identifying persons who have executed a CPR directive. Protocols adopted by the board of health shall include methods for rapid identification of persons who have executed a CPR directive, controlled distribution of the methods of identifying persons who have executed a CPR directive, and the information described in subsection (2) of this section. Nothing in this subsection (1) shall be construed to restrict any other manner in which a person may make a CPR directive.

(2) CPR directive protocols to be adopted by the state board shall require the following information concerning the person who is the subject of the CPR directive:
　　(a) The person's name, date of birth, and sex;
　　(b) The person's eye and hair color;
　　(c) The person's race or ethnic background;
　　(d) If applicable, the name of a hospice program in which the person is enrolled;
　　(e) The name, address, and telephone number of the person's attending physician;
　　(f) The person's signature or mark or, if applicable, the signature of a person authorized by this article to execute a CPR directive;
　　(g) The date on which the CPR directive form was signed;
　　(h) The person's directive concerning the administration of CPR, countersigned by the person's attending physician.
　　(i) The person's directive in the form of a document with a written statement as provided in section 12-34-105 (1) (c), C.R.S., or a statement in substantially similar form, indicating a decision regarding tissue donation. Such a document shall be executed in accordance with the provisions of the "Uniform Anatomical Gift Act", article 34 of title 12, C.R.S. Such a written statement may be in the following form:

I hereby make an anatomical gift, to be effective upon my death, of:
A.___ Any needed tissues
B.___ The following tissues:
　　___ Skin
　　___ Cornea
　　___ Bone, related tissues, and tendons
Donor signature: _____

15-18.6-104. Duty to comply with CPR directive - immunity - effect on criminal charges against another person.

(1) Emergency medical service personnel, health care providers, and health care facilities shall comply with a person's CPR directive that is apparent and immediately available. Any emergency medical service personnel, health care provider, health care facility, or any other person who, in good faith, complies with a CPR directive shall not be subject to civil or criminal liability or regulatory sanction for such compliance.

(2) Compliance by emergency medical service personnel, health care providers, or health care facilities with a CPR directive shall not affect the criminal prosecution of any person otherwise charged with the commission of a criminal act.

(3) In the absence of a CPR directive, a person's consent to CPR shall be presumed.

15-18.6-105. Effect of declaration after inpatient admission.

A CPR directive for any person who is admitted to a health care facility shall be implemented as a physician's order concerning resuscitation as directed by the person in the CPR directive, pending further physicians' orders.

15-18.6-106. Effect of CPR directive - absence - on life or health insurance.

Neither a CPR directive nor the failure of a person to execute one shall affect, impair, or modify any contract of life or health insurance or annuity or be the basis for any delay in issuing or refusing to issue an annuity or policy of life or health insurance or any increase of a premium therefore.

15-18.6-107. Revocation of CPR directive.

A CPR directive may be revoked at any time by a person who is the subject of such directive or by the agent or proxy decision-maker for such person. However, only those CPR directives executed originally by a guardian, agent, or proxy decision-maker may be revoked by a guardian, agent, or proxy decision-maker.

15-18.6-108. Effect of article on euthanasia - mercy killing - construction of statute.

Nothing in this article shall be construed as condoning, authorizing, or approving euthanasia or mercy killing. In addition, the general assembly does not intend that this article be construed as permitting any affirmative or deliberate act to end a person's life, except to permit natural death as provided by this article.

Living Will

The **living will** was established by the Colorado Medical Treatment Decision Act. This act affirms the right of a competent adult to accept or reject medical or surgical treatment. The Act further creates a procedure by which a competent adult may make such decisions in advance, before the adult becomes unconscious or otherwise incompetent to make such a decision. The Colorado Medical Treatment Decision Act is authorized in C.R.S. Title 15, Article 18, Part 1. Instructions for accessing statutes on the Internet are located in the Resource section of this manual. This statute is included at the end of this section of the manual.

Procedure for Creating a Living Will Declaration

Any competent adult may create a declaration as to medical or surgical treatment directing that life-sustaining procedures be withheld or withdrawn if, at some future time, he/she is in a terminal condition *and* either unconscious or otherwise incompetent to decide whether any medical procedure or intervention should be accepted or rejected. There are several procedures involved in developing a declaration. The following information provides an outline of the process. If questions arise about a living will, it is advisable to consult with the local county attorney regarding the specific legal issues pertaining to the pursuit of a living will declaration on behalf of an adult.

1) A **declaration must be completed** by the adult at a time when the adult has decisional capacity as it relates to his/her medical care.

   a. The "Declaration of Medical or Surgical Treatment" form, also known as a living will, may be used. This form can be found in the Resource section of this manual. Other standard living will forms may be used. A standard "living will" form developed for Colorado may be purchased from www.bradfordprinting.com.
   b. If the living will is written using a form other than the "Declaration of Medical or Surgical Treatment" form shown in the statute, it *should* include the following information:
      - A statement that the declarant, being of sound mind and at least 18 years of age, directs his/her life not be artificially prolonged when the declarant has become medically terminal.
      - Whether or not the declarant's life should be prolonged through artificial nutrition (for example, tube feeding) after the patient is medically terminal.
      - How long, if at all, artificial nutrition (for example, tube feeding) should be provided.
      - A statement that the declarant signs the declaration of his/her own free will.

c. If the living will is written using a form other than shown in statute, it *may* include a statement regarding organ and tissue donation and which organs, if any, may be donated upon the declarant's death.

2) If **artificial nutrition** is to be stopped, the living will must state this explicitly.

   a. If the living will does not specifically state that artificial nutrition is to be stopped, it will be continued as long as ordered by the attending physician.
   b. Even if the living will states that artificial nutrition is to be withheld, a physician may order that it be continued if necessary to relieve pain or provide comfort.

3) The adult must **sign the living will** in front of two witnesses and a Notary Public. Persons who may *not* witness the adult's signature are:

   a. Declarant's physician or any other physician
   b. Employee of the declarant's physician or of the health care facility where the adult is being treated
   c. Fellow patients in the care facility where the declarant is being treated
   d. Any person who believes he/she may be an heir to any portion of the declarant's estate
   e. Creditors

4) If the **declarant is unable to sign the declaration**, it may be signed by some other person at the declarant's direction and in the declarant's presence. However, the following people may *not* sign for the declarant:

   a. Declarant's physician or any other physician
   b. Employee of attending physician or of health care facility where declarant is a patient
   c. Person who has a claim against the declarant's estate or any person who believes he/she may be an heir to any portion of the declarant's estate
   d. Patient or resident of a health care facility where the declarant is a resident

Duties and Powers of the Physician in Implementing a Living Will

The physician plays a key role in implementing the terms of a living will declaration. The physician makes critical decisions as to the declarant's need for artificial nutrition, the confirmation of the declarant's terminal condition, the provision of appropriate notice to specified interested parties, and the implementation of the terms of the living will. Details of each of these and other physician duties and powers follow.

1) When a **physician receives a declaration** he/she shall:

   a. Determine if the declarant has a terminal condition.
   b. Request a second physician to examine the declarant to confirm or deny the terminal condition. If both physicians agree, they shall:
   - Certify the declarant's terminal condition in writing and enter the information into the declarant's medical record.
   - Place a copy of the declaration in the declarant's medical record.

2) The physician is responsible for signing a **certificate of terminal condition**.

3) The **attending physician shall** make immediate and reasonable efforts to **notify** the following persons (in the order presented) that a certificate of terminal condition has been signed:

   a. Declarant's spouse
   b. Declarant's adult child(ren)
   c. Declarant's parent
   d. Agent under a medical durable power of attorney

4) **Family or interested parties have 48 hours to challenge the validity** of the living will.

5) **If no challenge is filed** within 48 hours of the signing of the certificate of terminal condition, the treating physician may follow the terms of the declaration, i.e., the physician may remove artificial life support pursuant to the terms of the patient's living will.

6) The **physician may continue to provide artificial nutrition** in the event that he/she determines that discontinuation of artificial nutrition would result in pain or discomfort for the declarant. Only the smallest amount of artificial nutrition needed to alleviate pain and discomfort may be administered.

7) **The declarant may specify a time frame** in his/her living will regarding when artificial life support may be discontinued. The "Colorado Medical Treatment Decision Act" does not mandate a time frame. Even though the living will form found in the "Colorado Medical Treatment Decision Act" specifies that a declarant

who has been comatose or unconscious for a period of seven days or more must be removed from artificial life support, this time frame may be determined by the declarant.

Revoking or Challenging a Living Will

The right of the declarant to revoke a declaration is important. All copies of the declaration should be destroyed and all parties holding copies of the declaration should be notified by the declarant of its revocation. The declaration may be challenged through the court. Both revocation and challenges of the declaration are reviewed in more detail below.

1) The **declarant may revoke** a declaration at any time. The revocation may be made orally, in writing, or by means of burning, tearing, canceling, obliterating, or destroying the document.

2) The **validity of a living will declaration** under the Colorado Medical Treatment Decision Act may be challenged in the appropriate county court.

   a. The validity of the declaration may be challenged by:
      - Declarant's spouse
      - Declarant's adult child(ren)
      - Declarant's parent
      - Agent under a medical durable power of attorney
   b. Once a challenge has been filed, a temporary restraining order shall be issued to the attending physician.
   c. The court will appoint a guardian ad litem (GAL) for the declarant. The GAL will take action necessary and prudent for the declarant and will report to the court regarding the GAL's:
      - Actions
      - Findings
      - Conclusions
      - Recommendations
   d. The court may require evidence, including independent medical evidence.
   e. After a determination of the validity of the declaration, the court will enter an order stating its findings and decision.

Statutes Relating to the Medical Treatment Decision Act

The statutes included in this manual are listed below:

Title 15, Article 18, Part 1 Colorado Medical Treatment Decision Act

15-18-101. Short title.

This article shall be known and may be cited as the "Colorado Medical Treatment Decision Act."

15-18-102. Legislative declaration.

(1) The general assembly hereby finds, determines, and declares that:
    (a) Colorado law has traditionally recognized the right of a competent adult to accept or reject medical or surgical treatment affecting his person;
    (b) Recent advances in medical science have made it possible to prolong dying through the use of artificial, extraordinary, extreme, or radical medical or surgical procedures;
    (c) The use of such medical or surgical procedures increasingly involves patients who are unconscious or otherwise incompetent to accept or reject medical or surgical treatment affecting their persons;
    (d) The traditional right to accept or reject medical or surgical treatment should be available to an adult while he is competent, notwithstanding the fact that such medical or surgical treatment may be offered or applied when he is suffering from a terminal condition and is either unconscious or otherwise incompetent to decide whether such medical or surgical treatment should be accepted or rejected;

(e) This article affirms the traditional right to accept or reject medical or surgical treatment affecting one's person, and creates a procedure by which a competent adult may make such decisions in advance, before he becomes unconscious or otherwise incompetent to do so;

(f) It is the legislative intent that nothing in this article shall have the effect of modifying or changing currently practiced medical ethics or protocol with respect to any patient in the absence of a declaration as provided for in section 15-18-104;

(g) It is the legislative intent that nothing in this article shall require any person to execute a declaration.

15-18-103. Definitions.

As used in this article, unless the context otherwise requires:

(1) "Adult" means any person eighteen years of age or older.

(1.5) "Artificial nourishment" means nourishment supplied through a tube inserted into the stomach or intestines or nutrients injected intravenously into the bloodstream.

(2) "Attending physician" means the physician, whether selected by or assigned to a patient, who has primary responsibility for the treatment and care of said patient.

(3) "court" means the district court of the county in which a declarant having a terminal condition is located at the time of commencement of a proceeding pursuant to this article or, in the city and county of Denver, the probate court.

(4) "Declarant" means a mentally competent adult who executes a declaration.

(5) "Declaration" means a written document voluntarily executed by a declarant in accordance with the requirements of section 15-18-104.

(6) "Hospital" means an institution holding a license or certificate of compliance as a hospital issued by the department of public health and environment of this state and includes hospitals operated by the federal government in Colorado.

(7) "Life-sustaining procedure" means any medical procedure or intervention that, if administered to a qualified patient, would serve only to prolong the dying process. "Life-sustaining procedure" shall not include any medical procedure or intervention for nourishment of the qualified patient or considered necessary by the attending physician to provide comfort or alleviate pain. However, artificial nourishment may be withdrawn or withheld pursuant to section 15-18-104 (2.5).

(8) "Physician" means a person duly licensed under the provisions of article 36 of title 12, C.R.S.

(9) "Qualified patient" means a patient who has executed a declaration in accordance with this article and who has been certified by the attending physician and one other physician to be in a terminal condition.

(10) "Terminal condition" means an incurable or irreversible condition for which the administration of life-sustaining procedures will serve only to postpone the moment of death.

15-18-104. Declaration as to medical treatment.

(1) Any competent adult may execute a declaration directing that life-sustaining procedures be withheld or withdrawn if, at some future time, he is in a terminal condition and either unconscious or otherwise incompetent to decide whether any medical procedure or intervention should be accepted or rejected. It shall be the responsibility of the declarant or someone acting for him to submit the declaration to the attending physician for entry in the declarant's medical record.

(2) In the case of a declaration of a qualified patient known to the attending physician to be pregnant, a medical evaluation shall be made as to whether the fetus is viable and could with a reasonable degree of medical certainty develop to live birth with continued application of life-sustaining procedures. If such is the case, the declaration shall be given no force or effect.

(2.5)   a) The declarant may provide in his declaration that, in the event that the only procedure being provided is artificial nourishment, one of the following actions shall be taken:
            (I) That artificial nourishment not be continued when it is the only procedure being provided; or
            (II) That artificial nourishment be continued for a specified period of time when it is the only procedure being provided; or
            (III) That artificial nourishment be continued when it is the only procedure being provided.
         (b) A declaration executed prior to March 29, 1989, may be amended by a codicil to include the provisions of this subsection (2.5).

(2.6) Notwithstanding the provisions of subsection (2.5) of this section and section 15-18-103 (7), when an attending physician has determined that pain results from a discontinuance of artificial nourishment, he may order that such nourishment be provided but only to the extent necessary to provide comfort and alleviate such pain.

(3) A declaration executed before two witnesses by any competent adult shall be legally effective for the purposes of this article and may, but need not, be in the following form:

Declaration As To Medical Or Surgical Treatment

I, (name of declarant), being of sound mind and at least eighteen years of age, direct that my life shall not be artificially prolonged under the circumstances set forth below and hereby declare that:

1. If at any time my attending physician and one other qualified physician certify in writing that:

    a. I have an injury, disease, or illness which is not curable or reversible and which, in their judgment, is a terminal condition, and

    b. For a period of seven consecutive days or more, I have been unconscious, comatose, or otherwise incompetent so as to be unable to make or communicate responsible decisions concerning my person, then

I direct that, in accordance with Colorado law, life-sustaining procedures shall be withdrawn and withheld pursuant to the terms of this declaration, it being understood that life-sustaining procedures shall not include any medical procedure or intervention for nourishment considered necessary by the attending physician to provide comfort or alleviate pain. However, I may specifically direct, in accordance with Colorado law, that artificial nourishment be withdrawn or withheld pursuant to the terms of this declaration.

  2. In the event that the only procedure I am being provided is artificial nourishment, I direct that one of the following actions be taken:

    (initials of declarant) a. Artificial nourishment shall not be continued when it is the only procedure being provided; or

    (initials of declarant) b. Artificial nourishment shall be continued for _____ days when it is the only procedure being provided; or

    (initials of declarant) c. Artificial nourishment shall be continued when it is the only procedure being provided.

3. I execute this declaration, as my free and voluntary act, this _____ day of _____, 20___.

    By_____

    Declarant

The foregoing instrument was signed and declared by _____ to be his declaration, in the presence of us, who, in his presence, in the presence of each other, and at his request, have signed our names below as witnesses, and we declare that, at the time of the execution of this instrument, the declarant, according to our best knowledge and belief, was of sound mind and under no constraint or undue influence.

Dated at _____, Colorado, this _____ day of _____, 20___.

_____

    Name and Address

_____

    Name and Address

STATE OF COLORADO   )

County of _____)

    SUBSCRIBED and sworn to before me by _____, the declarant, and _____ and _____, witnesses, as the voluntary act and deed of the declarant this _____ day of _____, 20___.

My commission expires:

_____

Notary Public

(4) Any declaration made pursuant to subsection (3) of this section may also have a document with a written statement as provided in section 12-34-105 (1) (c), C.R.S., or a written statement in substantially similar form, indicating a decision regarding organ and tissue donation. Such a document shall be executed in accordance with the provisions of the "Uniform Anatomical Gift Act", article 34 of title 12, C.R.S. Such a written statement may be in the following form:

I hereby make an anatomical gift, to be effective upon my death, of:
    A.____ Any needed organs/tissues
    B.____ The following organs/tissues:

_____

Donor signature: _____

15-18-105. Inability of declarant to sign.

(1) In the event that the declarant is physically unable to sign the declaration, it may be signed by some other person in the declarant's presence and at his direction. Such other person shall not be:
    (a) The attending physician or any other physician; or
    (b) An employee of the attending physician or health care facility in which the declarant is a patient; or
    (c) A person who has a claim against any portion of the estate of the declarant at his death at the time the declaration is signed; or
    (d) A person who knows or believes that he is entitled to any portion of the estate of the declarant upon his death either as a beneficiary of a will in existence at the time the declaration is signed or as an heir at law.

15-18-106. Witnesses.

(1) The declaration shall be signed by the declarant in the presence of two witnesses. Said witnesses shall not include any person specified in section 15-18-105.

(2) If the declarant is a patient or resident of a health care facility, the witnesses shall not be patients of that facility.

15-18-107. Withdrawal - withholding of life-sustaining procedures.

In the event that an attending physician is presented with an unrevoked declaration executed by a declarant whom the physician believes has a terminal condition, the attending physician shall cause the declarant to be examined by one other physician. If both physicians find that the declarant has a terminal condition, they shall certify such fact in writing and enter such in the qualified patient's medical record of the hospital in which the withholding or withdrawal of life-sustaining procedures may occur, together with a copy of the declaration. If the attending physician has actual knowledge of the whereabouts of the qualified patient's spouse, any of his adult children, a parent, or attorney-in-fact under a durable power of attorney, the attending physician shall immediately make a reasonable effort to notify at least one of said persons, in the order named, that a certificate of terminal condition has been signed. If no action to challenge the validity of a declaration has been filed within forty-eight consecutive hours after the certification is made by the physicians, the attending physician shall then withdraw or withhold all life-sustaining procedures pursuant to the terms of the declaration.

15-18-108. Determination of validity.

(1) Any person who is the parent, adult child, spouse, or attorney-in-fact under a durable power of attorney of the qualified patient may challenge the validity of a declaration in the appropriate court of the county in which the qualified patient is located. Upon the filing of a petition to challenge the validity of a declaration and notification to the attending physician, a temporary restraining order shall be issued until a final determination as to validity is made.

(2)   (a) In proceedings pursuant to this section, the court shall appoint a guardian ad litem for the qualified patient, and the guardian ad litem shall take such action as he deems necessary and prudent in the best interest of the qualified patient and shall present to the court a report of his actions, findings, conclusions, and recommendations.

(b)   (I) Unless the court for good cause shown provides for a different method or time of notice, the petitioner, at least five days prior to the hearing, shall cause notice of the time and place of hearing to be given as follows:

(A) To the qualified patient's guardian or conservator, if any, and the court-appointed guardian ad litem; and

(B) To the qualified patient's spouse, if the identity and whereabouts of the spouse are known, to the petitioner, or otherwise to an adult child or parent of the qualified patient.

(II) Notice as required in this paragraph (b) shall be made in accordance with the Colorado rules of civil procedure.

(c) The court may require such evidence, including independent medical evidence, as it deems necessary.

(3) Upon a determination of the validity of the declaration, the court shall enter any appropriate order.

15-18-109. Revocation of declaration.

A declaration may be revoked by the declarant orally, in writing, or by burning, tearing, cancelling, obliterating, or destroying said declaration.

15-18-110. Liability.

(1) With respect to any declaration which appears on its face to have been executed in accordance with the requirements of this article:

(a) Any physician may act in compliance with such declaration in the absence of actual notice of revocation, fraud, misrepresentation, or improper execution;

(b) No physician signing a certificate of terminal condition or withholding or withdrawing life-sustaining procedures in compliance with a declaration shall be subject to civil liability, criminal penalty, or licensing sanctions therefor;

(c) No hospital or person acting under the direction of a physician and participating in the withholding or withdrawal of life-sustaining procedures in compliance with a declaration shall be subject to civil liability, criminal penalty, or licensing sanctions therefor.

15-18-111. Determination of suicide or homicide - effect of declaration on insurance.

The withholding or withdrawal of life-sustaining procedures from a qualified patient pursuant to this article shall not, for any purpose, constitute a suicide or a homicide. The existence of a declaration shall not affect, impair, or modify any contract of life insurance or annuity or be the basis for any delay in issuing or refusing to issue an annuity or policy of life insurance or any increase of the premium therefore. No insurer or provider of health care shall require any person to execute a declaration as a condition of being insured for or receiving health care services; nor shall the failure to execute a declaration be the basis for any increased or additional premium for a contract or policy for medical or health insurance.

15-18-112. Application of article.

(1) Nothing in this article shall be construed as altering or amending the standards of the practice of medicine or establishing any presumption, absent a valid declaration, nor as condoning, authorizing, or approving euthanasia or mercy killing, nor as permitting any affirmative or deliberate act or omission to end life, except to permit natural death as provided in this article.

(2) In the event of any conflict between the provisions of this article, or a declaration executed under this article, and the provisions of section 15-14-501, the provisions of this article and the declaration shall prevail.

15-18-113. Penalties.

(1) Any person who willfully conceals, defaces, damages, or destroys a declaration of another, without the knowledge and consent of the declarant, commits a class 1 misdemeanor and shall be punished as provided in section 18-1.3-501, C.R.S.

(2) Any person who falsifies or forges a declaration of another commits a class 5 felony and shall be punished as provided in section 18-1.3-401, C.R.S.

(3) Any person who falsifies or forges a declaration of another, and the terms of the declaration are carried out, resulting in the death of the purported declarant, commits a class 2 felony and shall be punished as provided in section 18-1.3-401, C.R.S.

(4) Any person who willfully withholds information concerning the revocation of the declaration of another commits a class 1 misdemeanorand shall be punished as provided in section 18-1.3-501, C.R.S.

(5) An attending physician who refuses to comply with the terms of a declaration valid on its face shall transfer the care of the declarant to another physician who is willing to comply with the declaration. Refusal of an attending physician to comply with a declaration and failure to transfer the care of the declarant to another physician shall constitute unprofessional conduct as defined in section 12-36-117, C.R.S.

Source: L. 85: Entire article added, p. 613, § 1, effective May 9. L. 89: (2) amended, p. 827, § 33, effective July 1. L. 2002: (1), (2), (3), and (4) amended, p. 1489, § 128, effective October 1.

Medical Durable Power of Attorney

With a **medical durable power of attorney (MDPOA),** the principal grants the agent authority to make medical treatment decisions on behalf of the principal should the principal lose decisional capacity. Such medical treatment includes artificial nourishment and hydration. The term "durable" refers to the fact that this form of POA *remains in effect* should the principal lose decisional capacity. The principal may include in the medical durable power of attorney agency instrument any directive, condition, or limitation of the agent's authority.

Procedure for Creating a Medical Durable Power of Attorney

1) The principal, or an attorney on behalf of the principal, may develop the written power of attorney document.

2) The principal determines the scope of authority for the agent under a medical durable power of attorney.

3) Medical durable power of attorney forms are available through attorneys' offices, in the "Your Right to Make Health Care Decisions" at hospitals and nursing homes, through the Guardianship Alliance of Colorado, and in some office supply stores. Forms may also be found at Bradford Forms Publishing on the Internet at www.bradfordpublishing.com under "Personal Property and Miscellaneous Forms."

4) Notarization and witnessing of the signing of medical durable power of attorney documents is highly recommended, but is not required in Colorado.

5) If questions arise regarding the specific authority given to an agent, it is advisable to consult with the local county attorney, or other objective attorney, and request a review of the agency instrument.

6) *Please note that a medical durable power of attorney may be referred to merely as a "POA." It is essential that the actual POA document (agency instrument) be reviewed to clarify the extent and type of authority given to the agent.*

Duties and Powers of Agents under a Medical Durable Power Of Attorney

The medical durable power of attorney (MDPOA) authorization requires:

1) The MDPOA agent to **act on behalf of the principal** in consenting to or refusing medical treatment, including artificial nourishment (for example, tube feeding) and hydration.

2) **When the principal has a guardian and/or conservator:**

   a. The agent maintains the POA given to him/her by the principal, unless guardian or conservator appointment states otherwise.
   b. A guardian cannot revoke a medical durable power of attorney without a court order.
   c. The MDPOA agent's healthcare decision takes precedence over that of a guardian.
   d. A guardian has recourse through the court to remove an agent who:
      - Becomes incapacitated
      - Refuses to serve
      - Is not acting according to instructions contained in the MDPOA agency instrument
      - Is not acting according to verbal or otherwise known instructions of the principal
      - Causes or threatens harm to the principal through action or inaction

Changing or Revoking Medical Durable Powers of Attorney

A medical durable power of attorney may be revoked or changed at any time by the principal. The original agency instrument that has been distributed should be destroyed and replaced with the new or revised agency instrument, if applicable.

1) The principal may choose to change or revoke a MDPOA designation if:

   a. The principal believes that the existing agent is no longer making decisions in the best interest of the principal.
   b. The principal decides that it is no longer necessary to have an agent because the POA was designated due to a special event or circumstance.
   c. The principal's spouse serves as agent, and the couple divorces or is granted a legal separation.

2) If the principal dies, the agent's authority under the agency instrument automatically terminates.

Statutes Relating to Medical Durable Power of Attorney

The statutes included in this manual are listed below:

Title 15, Article 14, Part 5 Powers Of Attorney

15-14-501. When power of attorney not affected by disability.

(1) Whenever a principal designates another his attorney-in-fact or agent by a power of attorney in writing and the writing contains the words "This power of attorney shall not be affected by disability of the principal." or "This power of attorney shall become effective upon the disability of the principal." or similar words showing the intent of the principal that the authority conferred shall be exercisable notwithstanding his disability, the authority of the attorney-in-fact or agent is exercisable by him as provided in the power on behalf of the principal notwithstanding later disability or incapacity of the principal at law or later uncertainty as to whether the principal is dead or alive. The authority of the attorney-in-fact or agent to act on behalf of the principal shall be set forth in the power and may relate to any act, power, duty, right, or obligation which the principal has or after acquires relating to the principal or any matter, transaction, or property, real or personal, tangible or intangible. The authority of the agent with regard to medical treatment decisions on behalf of a principal is set forth in sections 15-14-503 to 15-14-509. The attorney-in-fact or agent, however, is subject to the same limitations imposed upon court-appointed guardians contained in section 15-14-312 (1) (a). Additionally, the principal may expressly empower his attorney-in-fact or agent to renounce and disclaim interests and powers, to make gifts, in trust or otherwise, and to release and exercise powers of appointment. All acts done by the attorney-in-fact or agent pursuant to the power during any period of disability or incompetence or uncertainty as to whether the principal is dead or alive have the same effect and inure to the benefit of and bind the principal or his heirs, devisees, and personal representative as if the principal were alive, competent, and not disabled. If a guardian or conservator thereafter is appointed for the principal, the attorney-in-fact or agent, during the continuance of the appointment, shall consult with the guardian on matters concerning

the principal's personal care or account to the conservator on matters concerning the principal's financial affairs. The conservator has the same power the principal would have had if he were not disabled or incompetent to revoke, suspend, or terminate all or any part of the power of attorney or agency as it relates to financial matters. Subject to any limitation or restriction of the guardian's powers or duties set forth in the order of appointment and endorsed on the letters of guardianship, a guardian has the same power to revoke, suspend, or terminate all or any part of the power of attorney or agency as it relates to matters concerning the principal's personal care that the principal would have had if the principal were not disabled or incompetent, except with respect to medical treatment decisions made by an agent pursuant to sections 15-14-506 to 15-14-509; however, such exception shall not preclude a court from removing an agent in the event an agent becomes incapacitated, or is unwilling or unable to serve as an agent.

(2) An affidavit, executed by the attorney-in-fact or agent, stating that he did not have, at the time of doing an act pursuant to the power of attorney, actual knowledge of the termination of the power of attorney by death is, in the absence of fraud, conclusive proof of the nontermination of the power at that time. If the exercise of the power requires execution and delivery of any instrument which is recordable, the affidavit when authenticated for record is likewise recordable.

15-14-502. Other powers of attorney not revoked until notice of death or disability.

(1) The death, disability, or incompetence of any principal who has executed a power of attorney in writing, other than a power as described by section 15-14-501, does not revoke or terminate the agency as to the attorney-in-fact, agent, or other person who, without actual knowledge of the death, disability, or incompetence of the principal, acts in good faith under the power of attorney or agency. Any action so taken, unless otherwise invalid or unenforceable, binds the principal and his heirs, devisees, and personal representatives.

(2) An affidavit, executed by the attorney-in-fact or agent, stating that he did not have, at the time of doing an act pursuant to the power of attorney, actual knowledge of the revocation or termination of the power of attorney by death, disability, or incompetence is, in the absence of fraud, conclusive proof of the nonrevocation or nontermination of the power at that time. If the exercise of the power requires execution and delivery of any instrument which is recordable, the affidavit when authenticated for record is likewise recordable.

(3) This section shall not be construed to alter or affect any provision for revocation or termination contained in the power of attorney.

(4) All powers of attorney executed for real estate and other purposes, pursuant to law, shall be deemed valid until revoked as provided in the terms of the power of attorney or as provided by law.

15-14-503. Short title.

Sections 15-14-503 to 15-14-509 shall be known and may be cited as the "Colorado Patient Autonomy Act".

15-14-504. Legislative declaration - construction of statute.

(1) The general assembly hereby finds, determines, and declares that:
(a) Colorado law recognizes the right of an adult to accept or reject medical treatment and artificial nourishment and hydration;
(b) Each adult has the right to establish, in advance of the need for medical treatment, any directives and instructions for the administration of medical treatment in the event the person lacks the decisional capacity to provide informed consent to or refusal of medical treatment; and
(c) The enactment of a "Colorado Patient Autonomy Act" is appropriate to affirm a patient's autonomy in accepting or rejecting medical treatment, which right includes the making of medical treatment decisions through an appointed agent under a medical durable power of attorney.

(2) The general assembly does not intend to encourage or discourage any particular medical treatment or to interfere with or affect any method of religious or spiritual healing otherwise permitted by law.

(3) The general assembly does not intend that this part 5 be construed to restrict any other manner in which a person may make advance medical directives.

(4) Nothing in this part 5 shall be construed as condoning, authorizing, or approving euthanasia or mercy killing. In addition, the general assembly does not intend that this part 5 be construed as permitting any affirmative or deliberate act to end a person's life, except to permit natural death as provided by this part 5.

15-14-505. Definitions.

As used in sections 15-14-503 to 15-14-509, unless the context otherwise requires:

(1) "Adult" means any person eighteen years of age or older.

(2) "Advance medical directive" means any written instructions concerning the making of medical treatment decisions on behalf of the person who has provided the instructions. An advance medical directive includes a medical durable power of attorney executed pursuant to section 15-14-506, a declaration executed pursuant to the "Colorado Medical Treatment Decision Act", article 18 of this title, a power of attorney granting medical treatment authority executed prior to July 1, 1992, pursuant to section 15-14-501, and a declaration executed pursuant to article 18.6 of this title.

(3) "Artificial nourishment and hydration" means any medical procedure whereby nourishment or hydration is supplied through a tube inserted into a person's nose, mouth, stomach, or intestines or nutrients or fluids are injected intravenously into a person's bloodstream.

(4) "Decisional capacity" means the ability to provide informed consent to or refusal of medical treatment.

(5) "Health care facility" means any hospital, hospice, nursing facility, care center, dialysis treatment facility, assisted living facility, any entity that provides home and community-based services, home health care agency, or any other facility administering or contracting to administer medical treatment, and which is licensed, certified, or otherwise authorized or permitted by law to administer medical treatment.

(6) "Health care provider" means any physician or any other individual who administers medical treatment to persons and who is licensed, certified, or otherwise authorized or permitted by law to administer medical treatment or who is employed by or acting for such authorized person. Health care provider includes a health maintenance organization licensed and conducting business in this state.

(7) "Medical treatment" means the provision, withholding, or withdrawal of any health care, medical procedure, including artificially provided nourishment and hydration, surgery, cardiopulmonary resuscitation, or service to maintain, diagnose, treat, or provide for a patient's physical or mental health or personal care.

15-14-506. Medical durable power of attorney.

(1) The authority of an agent to act on behalf of the principal in consenting to or refusing medical treatment, including artificial nourishment and hydration, may be set forth in a medical durable power of attorney. A medical durable power of attorney may include any directive, condition, or limitation of an agent's authority.

(2) The agent shall act in accordance with the terms, directives, conditions, or limitations stated in the medical durable power of attorney, and in conformance with the principal's wishes that are known to the agent. If the medical durable power of attorney contains no directives, conditions, or limitations relating to the principal's medical condition, or if the principal's wishes are not otherwise known to the agent, the agent shall act in accordance with the best interests of the principal as determined by the agent.

(3) An agent appointed in a medical durable power of attorney may provide informed consent to or refusal of medical treatment on behalf of a principal who lacks decisional capacity and shall have the same power to make medical treatment decisions the principal would have if the principal did not lack such decisional capacity. An agent appointed in a medical durable power of attorney shall be considered a designated representative of the patient and shall have the same rights of access to the principal's medical records as the principal. In making medical treatment decisions on behalf of the

principal, and subject to the terms of the medical durable power of attorney, the agent shall confer with the principal's attending physician concerning the principal's medical condition.

(3.5) Any medical durable power of attorney executed under sections 15-14-503 to 15-14-509 may also have a document with a written statement as provided in section 12-34-105 (1) (c), C.R.S., or a statement in substantially similar form, indicating a decision regarding organ and tissue donation. Such a document shall be executed in accordance with the provisions of the "Uniform Anatomical Gift Act", article 34 of title 12, C.R.S. Such a written statement may be in the following form:

I hereby make an anatomical gift, to be effective upon my death, of:
A.____ Any needed organs/tissues
B.____ The following organs/tissues:

_____

Donor signature: _____

(4)   (a) Nothing in this section or in a medical durable power of attorney shall be construed to abrogate or limit any rights of the principal, including the right to revoke an agent's authority or the right to consent to or refuse any proposed medical treatment, and no agent may consent to or refuse medical treatment for a principal over the principal's objection.
(b) Nothing in this article shall be construed to supersede any provision of article 1 of title 25, C.R.S., article 10 of title 27, C.R.S., or article 10.5 of title 27, C.R.S.

(5)   (a) Nothing in this part 5 shall have the effect of modifying or changing the standards of the practice of medicine or medical ethics or protocols.
(b) Nothing in this part 5 or in a medical durable power of attorney shall be construed to compel or authorize a health care provider or health care facility to administer medical treatment that is otherwise illegal, medically inappropriate, or contrary to any federal or state law.
(c) Unless otherwise expressly provided in the medical durable power of attorney under which the principal appointed the principal's spouse as the agent, a subsequent divorce, dissolution of marriage, annulment of marriage, or legal separation between the principal and spouse appointed as agent automatically revokes such appointment. However, nothing in this paragraph (c) shall be construed to revoke any remaining provisions of the medical durable power of attorney.
(d) Unless otherwise specified in the medical durable power of attorney, if a principal revokes the appointment of an agent or the agent is unable or unwilling to serve, the appointment of the agent shall be revoked. However, nothing in this paragraph (d) shall be construed to revoke any remaining provisions of the medical durable power of attorney.

(6)   (a) This part 5 shall apply to any medical durable power of attorney executed on or after July 1, 1992. Nothing in this part 5 shall be construed to modify or affect

the terms of any durable power of attorney executed before such date and which grants medical treatment authority. Any such previously executed durable power of attorney may be amended to conform to the provisions of this part 5. In the event of a conflict between a medical durable power of attorney executed pursuant to this part 5 and a previously executed durable power of attorney, the provisions of the medical durable power of attorney executed pursuant to this part 5 shall prevail.

(b) Unless otherwise specified in a medical durable power of attorney, nothing in this part 5 shall be construed to modify or affect the terms of a declaration executed in accordance with the "Colorado Medical Treatment Decision Act", article 18 of this title.

15-14-507. Transfer of principal.

(1) A health care provider or health care facility shall provide notice to a principal and an agent of any policies based on moral convictions or religious beliefs of the health care provider or health care facility relative to the withholding or withdrawal of medical treatment. Notice shall be provided, when reasonably possible, prior to the provision of medical treatment or prior to or upon the admission of the principal to the health care facility, or as soon as possible thereafter.

(2) A health care provider or health care facility shall provide for the prompt transfer of the principal to another health care provider or health care facility if such health care provider or health care facility wishes not to comply with an agent's medical treatment decision on the basis of policies based on moral convictions or religious beliefs.

(3) An agent may transfer the principal to the care of another health care provider or health care facility if an attending physician or health care facility does not wish to comply with an agent's decision for any reason other than those described in subsection (1) of this section.

(4) The transfer of a principal to another health care provider or health care facility in accordance with the provisions of this section shall not constitute a violation of Title XIX of the federal "Social Security Act", 42 U.S.C., sec. 1395dd, regarding the transfer of patients.

(5) Nothing in this section shall relieve or exonerate an attending physician or health care facility from the duty to provide for the care and comfort of the principal pending transfer pursuant to this section.

15-14-508. Immunities.

(1) An agent or proxy-decision maker, as established in article 18.5 of this title, who acts in good faith in making medical treatment decisions on behalf of a principal pursuant to the terms of a medical durable power of attorney shall not be subject to civil or criminal liability therefor.

(2) Each health care provider and health care facility shall, in good faith, comply, in respective order, with the wishes of the principal, the terms of an advance medical directive, or the decision of an agent acting pursuant to an advance medical directive. A health care provider or health care facility which, in good faith, complies with the medical treatment decision of an agent acting in accordance with an advance medical directive shall not be subject to civil or criminal liability or regulatory sanction therefor.

(3) Good faith actions by any health care provider or health care facility in complying with a medical durable power of attorney or at the direction of a health care agent of the principal which result in the death of the principal following trauma caused by a criminal act or criminal conduct, shall not affect the criminal prosecution of any person charged with the commission of a criminal act or conduct.

(4) Neither a medical durable power of attorney nor the failure of a person to execute one shall affect, impair, or modify any contract of life or health insurance or annuity or be the basis for any delay in issuing or refusing to issue an annuity or policy of life or health insurance or any increase of a premium therefore.

15-14-509. Interstate effect of medical durable power of attorney.

(1) Unless otherwise stated in a medical durable power of attorney, it shall be presumed that the principal intends to have a medical durable power of attorney executed pursuant to this part 5 recognized to the fullest extent possible by the courts of any other state.

(2) Unless otherwise provided therein, any medical durable power of attorney or similar instrument executed in another state shall be presumed to comply with the provisions of this part 5 and may, in good faith, be relied upon by a health care provider or health care facility in this state.

Proxy Decision-Makers for Medical Treatment

The **Proxy Decision-Makers for Medical Treatment** statute affirms the traditional right of an adult to make his/her own medical treatment decisions, including decisions regarding artificial nutrition and hydration. This statute allows decisions to be made on behalf of an incapacitated adult should that adult lack the decisional capacity to provide informed consent. It describes the procedures involved in making decisions for adults who lack capacity to make decisions regarding medical treatment and artificial nutrition and hydration when there is no guardian or agent under a durable medical power of attorney. Should an incapacitated person refuse medical treatment only a guardian may override that decision. A proxy decision-maker for medical treatment is authorized in C.R.S. Title 15, Article 18.5, Part 1. Instructions for accessing statutes on the Internet are located in the Resource section of this manual. The statute is included at the end of this section of the manual.

Procedure for Appointing a Proxy Decision-Maker

In situations where an individual is hospitalized and in need of critical care and/or medical treatment decisions, but lacks such decisional capacity, someone else must be appointed the decision maker. Without a guardian or a medical durable power of attorney in place to make such decisions for the individual, a proxy decision maker may serve that function.

1) In a medical setting, **determination of decisional incapacity** can be made by the patient's physician. The court can also make this decision. Documentation must be entered into the patient's medical record includes the cause, nature and projected duration of the decisional incapacity.

2) A reasonable attempt must be made to provide **notice of the determination of the patient's incapacity** to make medical decisions. Individuals to whom notice must be provided are:

   a. The patient
   b. Patient's spouse
   c. Patient's parent
   d. Patient's adult child
   e. Patient's adult sibling
   f. Patient's adult grandchild
   g. Any adult close friend

3) Family members and interested persons must come to a consensus and **choose the interested person who will serve as the proxy decision maker**.

a. The proxy decision-maker should be someone who has a close relationship with the patient and is most likely to know the patient's wishes regarding medical treatment decisions.

b. If there is a disagreement as to who should serve as the proxy decision maker, then any interested person, with the exception of a government entity, may petition the court for guardianship of the adult. Government entities, such as county departments of social services, may NOT petition the court for guardianship as an interested party solely for the purpose of making medical treatment decisions. *However, the court may act on its own motion or on a petition filed by a third person to appoint the county department of social services as the guardian for the express purpose of making medical treatment decisions.* The county may then accept the guardianship appointment.

4) The attending physician or other health care provider must make a reasonable attempt to **notify the patient that a proxy decision-maker** will be appointed or has been appointed. The notice will inform the patient of the right to object to that proxy.

Duties and Powers of a Proxy Decision-Maker

1) The proxy decision maker will **make decisions as to artificial nutrition, hydration, and medical treatment**.

   a. Artificial nutrition and/or hydration can only be stopped when both the attending physician and a second, independent physician trained in neurology or neurosurgery, certify in the patient's medical record, that the provision or continuation of artificial nutrition and/or hydration will only prolong death and will not allow the patient to return to independent neurological functioning.
   b. When a proxy decision must be made as to medical treatment, the proxy or an interested party may request assistance from the hospital's medical ethics committee where the patient is located.

2) If any interested person, the proxy decision-maker, or the attending physician believes the patient has **regained decisional capacity,** a physician must re-examine the patient to make that determination.

   a. The determination, and the basis for the determination, must be entered into the patient's medical record.
   b. The attending physician will notify the:
   - Proxy decision-maker
   - Patient
   - Person who initiated the redetermination

Statutes Relating to Proxy Decision-Makers

The statutes included in this manual are listed below:

> 15-18.5-101. Legislative declaration - construction of statute.
> 15-18.5-102. Definitions applicable to medical durable power of attorney - applicability.
> 15-18.5-103. Proxy decision-makers for medical treatment authorized.

Title 15, Article 18.5, Part 1 Proxy Decision-Makers For Medical Treatment

15-18.5-101. Legislative declaration - construction of statute.

(1) The general assembly hereby finds, determines, and declares that:
> (a) All adult persons have a fundamental right to make their own medical treatment decisions, including decisions regarding medical treatment and artificial nourishment and hydration;
> (b) The lack of decisional capacity to provide informed consent to or refusal of medical treatment should not preclude such decisions from being made on behalf of a person who lacks such decisional capacity and who has no known advance medical directive, or whose wishes are not otherwise known; and
> (c) The enactment of legislation to authorize proxy decision-makers to make medical treatment decisions on behalf of persons lacking the decisional capacity to provide informed consent to or refusal of medical treatment is appropriate.

(2) The general assembly does not intend to encourage or discourage any particular medical treatment or to interfere with or affect any method of religious or spiritual healing otherwise permitted by law.

(3) Nothing in this article shall be construed as condoning, authorizing, or approving euthanasia or mercy killing. In addition, the general assembly does not intend that this article be construed as permitting any affirmative or deliberate act to end a person's life, except to permit natural death as provided by this article.

15-18.5-102. Definitions applicable to medical durable power of attorney - applicability.

(1) The definitions set forth in section 15-14-505 shall apply to the provisions of this article.

(2) The provisions of sections 15-14-506 to 15-14-509 shall apply to this article. In addition, proxy decision-makers, health care providers, and health care facilities shall be subject to the provisions of this article.

15-18.5-103. Proxy decision-makers for medical treatment authorized.

(1) A health care provider or health care facility may rely, in good faith, upon the medical treatment decision of a proxy decision-maker selected in accordance with subsection (4) of this section if an adult patient's attending physician determines that such patient lacks the decisional capacity to provide informed consent to or refusal of medical treatment and no guardian with medical decision-making authority, agent appointed in a medical durable power of attorney, or other known person has the legal authority to provide such consent or refusal on the patient's behalf.

(2) The determination that an adult patient lacks decisional capacity to provide informed consent to or refusal of medical treatment may be made by a court or the attending physician, and such determination shall be documented in such patient's medical record. The attending physician shall make specific findings regarding the cause, nature, and projected duration of the patient's lack of decisional capacity, which findings shall be included in the patient's medical record.

(3) Upon a determination that an adult patient lacks decisional capacity to provide informed consent to or refusal of medical treatment, the attending physician, or such physician's designee, shall make reasonable efforts to notify the patient of the patient's lack of decisional capacity. In addition, the attending physician, or such physician's designee, shall make reasonable efforts to locate as many interested persons as defined in this subsection (3) as practicable and the attending physician may rely on such individuals to notify other family members or interested persons. For the purposes of this section, "interested persons" means the patient's spouse, either parent of the patient, any adult child, sibling, or grandchild of the patient, or any close friend of the patient. Upon locating an interested person, the attending physician, or such physician's designee, shall inform such person of the patient's lack of decisional capacity and that a proxy decision-maker should be selected for the patient.

(4)   (a) It shall be the responsibility of the interested persons specified in subsection (3) of this section to make reasonable efforts to reach a consensus as to whom among them shall make medical treatment decisions on behalf of the patient. The person selected to act as the patient's proxy decision-maker should be the person who has a close relationship with the patient and who is most likely to be currently informed of the patient's wishes regarding medical treatment decisions. If any of the interested persons specified in subsection (3) of this section disagrees with the selection or the decision of the proxy decision-maker or, if, after reasonable efforts, the interested persons specified in subsection (3) of this section are unable to reach a consensus as to who should act as the proxy decision-maker, then any of the interested persons specified in subsection (3) of this section may seek guardianship of the patient by initiating guardianship proceedings pursuant to part 3 of article 14 of this title. Only said persons may initiate such proceedings with regard to the patient.

(b) Nothing in this section shall be construed to preclude any interested person described in subsection (3) of this section from initiating a guardianship proceeding pursuant to part 3 of article 14 of this title for any reason any time after said persons have conformed with paragraph (a) of this subsection (4).

(5) When an attending physician determines that an adult patient lacks decisional capacity, the attending physician or another health care provider shall make reasonable efforts to advise the patient of such determination, of the identity of the proxy decision-maker, and of the patient's right to object, pursuant to section 15-14-506 (4) (a).

(6) Artificial nourishment and hydration may be withheld or withdrawn from a patient upon a decision of a proxy only when the attending physician and a second independent physician trained in neurology or neurosurgery certify in the patient's medical record that the provision or continuation of artificial nourishment or hydration is merely prolonging the act of dying and is unlikely to result in the restoration of the patient to independent neurological functioning.

(6.5) The assistance of a health care facility's medical ethics committee shall be provided upon the request of a proxy decision-maker or any other interested person specified in subsection (3) of this section whenever the proxy decision-maker is considering or has made a decision to withhold or withdraw medical treatment. If there is no medical ethics committee for a health care facility, such facility may provide an outside referral for such assistance or consultation.

(7) If any of the interested persons specified in subsection (3) of this section or the guardian or the attending physician believes the patient has regained decisional capacity, then the attending physician shall reexamine the patient and determine whether or not the patient has regained such decisional capacity and shall enter the decision and the basis therefore into the patient's medical record and shall notify the patient, the proxy decision-maker, and the person who initiated the redetermination of decisional capacity.

(8) Except for a court acting on its own motion, no governmental entity, including the state department of human services and the county departments of social services, may petition the court as an interested person pursuant to part 3 of article 14 of this title. In addition, nothing in this article shall be construed to authorize the county director of any county department of social services, or designee of such director, to petition the court pursuant to section 26-3.1-104, C.R.S., in regard to any patient subject to the provisions of this article.

(9) Any attending physician, health care provider, or health care facility that makes reasonable attempts to locate and communicate with a proxy decision-maker shall not be subject to civil or criminal liability or regulatory sanction therefore.

Representative Payee

This section of the manual defines and describes key terms used when referring to **representative payee**, the procedures involved in the appointment of a representative payee, the duties of a representative payee, and how the beneficiary or someone else with good cause can change representative payees. Responding to allegations of abuse of representative payee authority is addressed in the final section of the manual.

Detailed information for organizations that are interested in representative payee responsibilities is found in the "Guide for Organizational Representative Payee" at www.ssa.gov/payee/newpubs.htm. The following (more general) information on representative payee issues is available on the Internet at www.ssa.gov/payee/index.htm or by calling 1-800-772-1213.

Terms used in reference to representative payee include:

- ➤ **"Beneficiary"** refers to the person who is eligible for and receiving Social Security Administration funds, either directly or through the services of a representative payee arrangement.
- ➤ **"Representative payee"** (rep payee) is an individual or organization that receives (or intercepts) payments for someone who cannot manage or direct the management of his/her money. Reference: Sections 205(j)(1) and 1631(a)(2)(A) of the Social Security Act.

Appointment of Individuals and Agencies as Representative Payee

When an adult beneficiary is determined incapable of managing or directing his/her own Social Security retirement benefits, Social Security Disability Income (SSDI), and/or Supplemental Security Income (SSI) payments, the Social Security Administration (SSA) may appoint a rep payee after careful investigation. A rep payee can be an individual, an agency, or an organization, such as county departments of social services or a nursing home. Having power of attorney (POA) authority over someone does not automatically qualify the agent as a rep payee. There is a separate application process to become a rep payee.

The SSA has teaching and support resources available to agencies that have assumed or may consider assuming the responsibilities of rep payee for vulnerable members of their respective communities. The Internet address to view and/or order these resources is www.ssa.gov/payee/training2.htm. The resources include materials entitled:

- "Lesson Plan"
- "Guide for Organizational Rep Payees"
- "The Difference Is You"

There are specific groups of beneficiaries that the law requires have a rep payee. These include:

1) Legally incompetent adults.

2) Adults with disabilities who are determined by SSA to be incapable of handling their benefits in a reasonable manner, and whom SSA has determined to have a drug addiction or alcohol (DAA) condition.

Procedure for Becoming a Representative Payee

Applying to be a Representative Payee

The designation of a rep payee is made using an application process through local Social Security offices. Form SSA-11 ("Request To Be Selected As Payee") is the federal application form used. The SSA requires this form be completed in a face-to-face interview with the applying Social Security beneficiary. Exceptions to this face-to-face interview requirement are made if the beneficiary is unable to appear in person, due to illness or disability. Organizations that are known to have a good working relationship with their local SSA office and are applying for designation as rep payee, may be permitted to do so over the phone. General information on rep payee application issues is available on the Internet at www.ssa.gov/payee/index.htm or by calling 1-800-772-1213.

Choosing Representative Payees

An individual may request to be designated as rep payee by submitting the SSA-11 application form to the local SSA office. The SSA will review the application form and will select someone who knows and wants to help the beneficiary. The **beneficiary may request to have a certain individual designated** as his/her rep payee, in which case the SSA will follow the same application and review process. Individuals most likely to be selected as rep payee are:

- Family members
- Friends
- Guardians or conservators
- Attorneys

Organizations are preferred rep payees for beneficiaries who have certain disabilities because such entities are often most aware of the special needs of these individuals and how financial resources can help to meet those needs. The SSA, local organizations, and agencies work together to establish good working relationships that provide optimal services to each beneficiary. The disability groups considered best served by organizational or agency involvement as rep payee are:

- Individuals with mental illnesses
- Individuals with substance abuse problems
- Individuals who are homeless

Organizations and agencies most likely to be selected as rep payee are:

- Social service agencies
- Nursing homes
- Other organizations that have established themselves as rep payees with SSA

Duties, Limitations, Accounting, and Fee Information
Effecting a Representative Payee

Duties

A rep payee is required to:

1) **Submit an annual report** that includes:

   a. How the beneficiary's payments were used.
   b. What portion of the beneficiary's payments (if any) were saved.
   c. A statement regarding the beneficiary's custody status, that is, whether or not the beneficiary remains the ward of a specific guardian or agency representative, remains single, and so forth. (Some state mental institutions may participate in an alternative monitoring program and are not required to report on this issue.)

2) **Establish an accounting system** that will track how much money was received, how much money was spent, and the balance saved for the beneficiary. (See details to follow in "Accounting System" section.)

3) **Monitor the beneficiary's needs and condition through regular contact** with the beneficiary and beneficiary's custodians.

4) **Monitor the beneficiary's current and foreseeable needs** in order to use benefits in the beneficiary's best interests. These needs include but are not limited to:

   a. Food
   b. Shelter
   c. Utilities
   d. Dental care
   e. Medical care and insurance
   f. Rehabilitation expenses
   g. Clothing
   h. Personal hygiene
   i. Education

5) **Consider providing the beneficiary with a small stipend for discretionary use**. Any remaining funds must be saved or invested in trust for the beneficiary.

6) **Apply the benefit payments** only for the beneficiary's use and benefit.

7) **Notify the local Social Security Administration (SSA) of any change** in the rep payee's circumstances that would affect performance of the payee responsibilities.

8) **Report to the local SSA any event that will affect the amount of benefits** the beneficiary receives.

9) **Turn over saved benefits** should the beneficiary die. Benefits should be given to the legal representative of the estate or otherwise handled according to state law.

   a. A Social Security check *is not* payable for the month of death (with the exception of an SSI check, even if the beneficiary dies on the last day of the month.
   b. Any check received for the month of death or later must be returned to SSA.
   c. An SSI check *is* payable for the month of death. However, any SSI checks that are received *after* the month of death must be returned to SSA.

Limitations

Rep payees are responsible for many aspects of the beneficiary's financial affairs. However, there are limitations on the rep payee's power. The rep payee may not:

1) Use funds for rep payee's personal expenses.

2) Put the beneficiary's funds in rep payee's or other person's account.

3) Use funds for anything other than the beneficiary's needs.

4) Keep conserved funds after termination of rep payee status.

5) Charge the beneficiary for services unless authorized by SSA.

6) Make medical decisions on behalf of the beneficiary.

7) Sign legal documents, other than Social Security documents, on behalf of a beneficiary.

8) Have legal authority over earned income, pensions, or any income from sources other than Social Security, SSDI, and/or SSI payments.

Accounting System

Rep payee organizations must keep an accurate and current account of the beneficiary's financial needs and the transactions taken by the rep payee organization on behalf of the beneficiary. A rep payee organization must establish an accounting system that will:

1) Track how much money was received.

2) Track how much money was spent.

3) Maintain the balance saved for each beneficiary.

4) Save financial records for at least two years and make them available to SSA upon request.

5) Provide reports that are understandable and up-to-date so SSA and the beneficiary know how the money is spent.

6) Prorate interest earned based on each beneficiary's portion of the balance.

7) Issue an alert to the rep payee when a SSI beneficiary's conserved benefits approach the resource limit set by SSA.

Fees for Representative Payee Services

Qualified agencies and organizations that serve as rep payee may only collect a monthly "fee for service" based upon expenses incurred in providing services performed as rep payee with authorization from the local SSA. Detailed information for organizations interested in obtaining rep payee authority for a beneficiary, including the process required to obtain permission to collect a fee for service, are available at www.ssa.gov/payee/newpubs.htm.

Individuals who serve as rep payees may not collect fees for this service.

Changing Representative Payee

Changes in rep payee become necessary for many reasons. If and when a change in rep payee is requested, the local SSA office will review the request and make necessary changes.

Representative Payee May Terminate Appointment

If the person, agency, or organization designated as rep payee wishes to terminate that appointment, the rep payee must:

1) Immediately notify the Social Security office.

2) Return any benefits, including interest and cash on hand to the Social Security Administration. (The returned assets will be reissued to the beneficiary or to the new rep payee.)

Beneficiary May Change Representative Payees

If the beneficiary wishes to make a change in rep payee, he/she must:

1) Tell the present rep payee that he/she plans to request a new rep payee.

2) Request that the new rep payee applicant file an SSA-11 application at a Social Security office.

Terminating Representative Payee

1) Beneficiaries may inform the SSA that he/she feels there is no longer a need for a rep payee. The beneficiary must provide proof to SSA that he/she is mentally and physically able to handle his/her SSA benefits by providing *one* of the following:

   a. A doctor's statement that there has been a change in condition and the beneficiary is now able to manage his/her own SSA benefits.
   b. An official copy of a court order saying that the court believes that the beneficiary can manage his/her own SSA benefits.
   c. Other evidence that shows the beneficiary's ability to manage his/her own SSA benefits.

2) If SSA believes the beneficiary's condition has improved that he/she no longer needs a rep payee, SSA may reevaluate the beneficiary's eligibility for continued SSA benefits.

Abuse of Authority

This section of the manual describes how to respond to allegations of abuse of guardianship, conservatorship, powers of attorney, and representative payee authority, defines terms used in proceedings that address such abuse of authority, and describes the procedures involved in addressing such situations.

The following terms regarding abuse of authority are used:

> ➤ **"Agent"** refers to the person assigned by the principal to assume the duties specified under a power of attorney.
> ➤ **"Agency"** refers to the relationship between the principal and the agent.
> ➤ **"Agency instrument"** refers to the written power of attorney document.
> ➤ **"Beneficiary"** refers to the person who is eligible for and receiving Social Security Administration funds, either directly or through the services of a representative payee arrangement.
> ➤ **"Guardian ad litem"** (GAL) is a person appointed by the court to take legal action on behalf of the respondent. The guardian ad litem is charged with representing and making recommendations that are in the respondent's best interest. (For more detailed information on GAL, read C.R.S. 15-10-403 (5), C.R.S. 15-14-115 and Rule 15, Colorado Rules of Probate Procedure.)
> ➤ **"Principal"** refers to the person giving power of attorney to another.
> ➤ **"Protected Person"** refers to the person for whom the conservatorship was granted by the court.
> ➤ **"Representative payee"** (rep payee) is an individual or organization that receives (or intercepts) payments for someone who cannot manage or direct the management of his/her money.
> ➤ **"Third party"** refers to a person or company requested by the agent to deal with a principal's property as authorized in the agency instrument.
> ➤ **"Ward"** refers to the person for whom the guardianship was granted by the court.

Abuse of Guardianship Authority

Abuse of guardianship authority occurs in several situations:

1) **A guardian takes advantage of the ward or neglects appointment responsibilities.** For example, a guardian may not be guaranteeing that the ward is receiving proper and adequate medical care.

2) The **guardian is unable to prudently exercise his/her authority**. For example, the guardian's capacity for decision-making becomes questionable.

3) The **assumption of authority is taken *without* legal authorization**. For example:

   a. A person may isolate an at-risk adult from other family members against the wishes of the adult, claiming that it is "for the good" of the adult.
   b. A person, claiming to be an adult's guardian, is not able to provide the court document(s) to confirm that appointment because such an appointment was never made.

4) A guardian has limited legal authority but **makes decisions beyond those included in the guardianship order**.

Abuse of authority creates a serious and potentially lethal situation for the at-risk adult. Additionally, professionals who might assist the abuse victim, such as nursing home staff members or law enforcement, may be unable to do so if they have incorrect or insufficient information as to the types, parameters, and requirements of guardianship authority granted by the court appointment.

Procedure to Address Abuse of Guardianship Authority

In situations of abuse of guardianship authority, a petition to the court should be filed for a temporary substitute guardianship (TSG). In emergency situations, the process for obtaining a temporary guardian for an at-risk adult is outlined in the *Guardianship* section of this manual. In all other cases, a petition should be filed for a TSG, as described below:

1) **Petition the court** to consider the appointment of a TSG.

2) The **ward or any other interested person may petition for removal of a guardian** on the grounds that removal would be in the best interest of the ward or for other good cause.

3) **Provide evidence** that the current guardian is not effectively performing court-ordered duties and that the welfare of the ward is at risk and/or requires immediate action.

4) The **court determines whether the presented evidence supports** the appointment of a TSG.

5) If the **court appoints a TSG,** the:

    a. Original guardian's authority is suspended during the TSG appointment
    b. TSG is appointed for up to 6 months
    c. TSG has the same authority as the original guardian, unless altered by the court
    d. TSG may have powers modified at any time
    e. TSG may be removed at any time
    f. TSG is subject to all provisions of Colorado Uniform Guardianship and Protective Proceedings Act
    g. TSG may be required to make reports to the court.

6) If notice was not otherwise provided, the **TSG must provide notice** of appointment within 5 days of the court order to the ward, guardian, and other interested persons.

Abuse of Conservatorship Authority

Abuse of conservatorship authority occurs in several situations:

1) A conservator takes **advantage of the protected person or neglects his/her responsibilities.** For example, a conservator is not making payments for the protected person's care.

2) The **conservator is unable to prudently exercise his/her authority**. For example, the conservator's financial transactions on behalf of the protected person are questionable.

3) The **assumption of conservatorship authority is taken *without* legal authorization**. For example, a relative may take over financial control of an adult's assets against the wishes of the adult, claiming that it is "for the good" of the adult. The relative, claiming to be the adult's conservator, is not able to provide the court document(s) to confirm that appointment because the appointment never occurred.

4) A conservator has limited legal authority but **makes decisions and financial transactions that are beyond the scope of the court order**. For example, a conservator has the legal authority to provide for payment for the care of an adult in a facility but invests the adult's assets in stock options.

Abuse of authority creates a serious and potentially harmful situation for the at-risk adult. Additionally, professionals who might assist the abuse victim, such as nursing home staff members or law enforcement, may be unable to do so if they have incorrect or insufficient information as to the types, parameters, and requirements of conservatorship authority granted by the court.

Procedure to Address Abuse of Conservatorship Authority

The protected person, or any other interested person, may petition the court at any time for the removal of a conservator on grounds that removal would be in the best interest of the protected person, or for other good cause. In situations of alleged abuse of conservatorship authority, the following procedure should be used when requesting a change in conservator:

1) **File a petition** in the appointing court for removal of the acting conservator and for the appointment of a temporary or successor conservator.

2) **Provide evidence** to the court that the current conservator is not effectively performing court-ordered duties, and that the welfare of the protected person and his/her estate requires immediate action.

3) The **court will determine whether evidence supports** the appointment of a temporary or successor conservator. The court may modify the type of the original appointment or the powers granted to the original conservator.

Abuse of Power of Attorney Authority

Abuse of power of attorney designation is a frequent form of authority abuse. Since there is no court oversight involved with POA, except in the rare cases where such involvement is specified within the agency instrument, accountability of the agent is sometimes difficult to enforce. Examples of abuse of power of attorney designation follow:

1) **An agent under a MDPOA assumes authority that goes beyond the scope of a MDPOA.** For example, a son with a MDPOA removes his mother from a nursing home against medical advice, in order to care for her at home, but is unable to or does not care for her adequately.

2) **An agent under a POA neglects the needs of the principal and** uses the principal's money for the agent's own benefit. For example, the agent purchases a new car and other personal items for herself, and neglects to pay the principal's monthly mortgage payments and utility bills.

3) **An agent under a POA that provides authority for financial transactions on behalf of the principal, neglects those duties.** For example, the agent neglects to pay the principal's ongoing nursing home costs, resulting in the threatened eviction of the principal from the facility.

Abuse of power of attorney designation, and fraudulent claims of such designation, create serious and potentially harmful situations for the principal. Professionals who might assist the at-risk adults, such as nursing home staff members or law enforcement, may be unable to do so if they have incorrect or insufficient information/knowledge as to the types, parameters, and requirements of power of attorney designations. *In each case, it is essential that the agency instrument (POA document) be examined to clarify the extent and type of authority given to the agent.*

Procedure to Address Abuse of Power of Attorney Authority

In situations of abuse of power of attorney (POA) authority, it is standard procedure to insist on reviewing the agency instrument to determine the extent of the authority delegated to an agent.

In all cases of POA authority abuse, the most expedient response is the principal's revocation or amendment of the POA. The following are some suggestions for best practice when working with a situation involving an agent under a POA:

1) **Scrutinize each POA arrangement carefully** to determine if there is a need for action.

2) **Consider each arrangement on its own merits** as to the agent and the agency instrument.

3) **Develop contingency plans with or for the principal** to implement after revocation. (Determine who will make financial and/or medical decisions.)

4) **Consider having a successor agent designated** under a new or amended agency instrument to assist, expedite, and minimize the expense of problems that could arise in the future, if the principal has capacity.

5) **Avoid engaging in undue influence** over a principal with diminished capacity. If the principal lacks capacity, it is prudent to seek court intervention.

6) **Ensure that the most appropriate level of authority is pursued**, such as proxy decision maker for medical treatment, conservator, and/or guardian, for a principal with diminished capacity.

The following methods can be used to revoke or amend a POA:

1) **Voluntary revocation and amendment** of agency instrument can be done by the principal in a number of ways including:

   a. Writing a revocation that is dated, signed by the principal, and recorded with the county clerk and recorder's office.
   b. Verbally informing all interested parties of the revocation or amendment of the agency instrument. (This is difficult to prove.)
   c. Preparing a new document and destroying the old document.
   d. Revoking or amending only the agent, only the agency instrument, or both.

2) **Imposed revocation or termination of POA** authority occurs upon the:

a. Death of the principal, but only if the agent has knowledge of the principal's death.
b. Divorce or legal separation of the agent (spouse) from the principal.
c. Finding by the court that the principal is unable to revoke or control an abusive and/or neglectful agent. (Interested persons, the agent, principal, guardian, or conservator may bring such issues before the court.)

Once the problem agent and/or agency instrument has been revoked or amended, consider what legal actions may be appropriate in each situation. Some options follow:

1) **Civil action through a private or pro bono attorney** may result in an order to the agent to return or give up illegally, unethically obtained goods, and/or pay a fine or surcharge commensurate with the level of abuse. Separate civil actions may be filed for:

   a. Breach of fiduciary duty
   b. Questionable or poor accounting practices
   c. Agent fraud
   d. Theft or misappropriation of funds

2) **Criminal prosecution through the district attorney's office.**

   a. District Attorneys are increasingly willing to become involved in protecting vulnerable adults.
   b. The Colorado Attorney General's office has become increasingly active and supportive.

3) **Referral of the situation to AARP ElderWatch,** a program that fights financial exploitation of the elderly. ElderWatch may be reached at 1-800-222-4444.

4) **Pursuit of guardianship or conservatorship**.

5) **Petition for an accounting to the court** of the agent's activities and/or the status of the principal's assets when there is a question about the agent's legal and/or ethical performance of duties.

6) **File a complaint with the district or probate court.**

   a. Request that the agent, or any other person, respond to concerns that the agent may have:
   - Concealed the principal's assets and pertinent information
   - Embezzled the principal's assets
   - Carried away or disposed of assets belonging to the principal
   - Held or concealed knowledge of deeds, bonds, contracts, or other writings which indicate title, interest, or claim of the protected person

b. Complaints may be filed by:
- Guardians
- Conservators
- Heirs
- Beneficiaries
- Creditors
- Others interested in the estate of any protected person

Statutes Relating to Abuse of Power of Attorney

The following statutes pertain to the abuse of powers of attorney.

15-14-418 – General Duties of Conservator, Financial Plan
15-14-604 – Duration Of Agency – Amendment And Revocation – Effect Of
Disability – Resignation Of Agent
15-14-605 – Dissolution of Marriage
15-14-606 – Duty of Agent – Standard of Care
15-14-609 – Agency – court Relationship
15-16-302 – Trustee's Standard of Care and Performance

15-14-418. General duties of conservator - financial plan.

(1) A conservator, in relation to powers conferred by this part 4 or implicit in the title acquired by virtue of the proceeding, is a fiduciary and shall observe the standards of care applicable to a trustee.

(2) A conservator shall take into account the limitations of the protected person, and to the extent possible, as directed by the order of appointment or the financial plan, encourage the person to participate in decisions, act in the person's own behalf, and develop or regain the ability to manage the person's estate and business affairs.

(3) Within a time set by the court, but no later than ninety days after appointment, a conservator shall file for approval with the appointing court a financial plan for protecting, managing, expending, and distributing the income and assets of the protected person's estate. The financial plan shall be based upon a comparison of the projected income and expenses of the protected person and shall set forth a plan to address the needs of the person and how the assets and income of the protected person shall be managed to meet those needs. The financial plan must be based on the actual needs of the person and take into consideration the best interest of the person. The conservator shall include in the financial plan steps to the extent possible to develop or restore the person's ability to manage the person's property, an estimate of the duration of the conservatorship, and projections of expenses and resources.

(4) In investing an estate, selecting assets of the estate for distribution, and invoking powers of revocation or withdrawal available for the use and benefit of the protected person and exercisable by the conservator, a conservator shall take into account any estate plan of the person known to the conservator. The conservator may examine the will and any other donative, nominative, or other appointive instrument of the person.

(5) A conservator shall file an amended financial plan whenever there is a change in circumstances that requires a substantial deviation from the existing financial plan.

15-14-604. Duration of agency - amendment and revocation - effect of disability - resignation of agent.

(1) Where an agency instrument contains the language specified in section 15-14-501 (1) or otherwise specifies that the agent designated therein may exercise the authority conferred notwithstanding the principal's disability, such agent may exercise such authority notwithstanding the principal's later disability or incapacity or later uncertainty as to whether the principal is dead.

(2) Any agency created by an agency instrument continues until the death of the principal, regardless of the length of time that elapses, unless the agency instrument states an earlier termination date. The principal may amend or revoke the agency instrument at any time and in any manner that is communicated to the agent or to any other person who is related to the subject matter of the agency. Any agent who acts in good faith on behalf of the principal within the scope of an agency instrument is not liable for any acts that are no longer authorized by reason of an amendment or revocation of the agency instrument until the agent receives actual notice of the amendment or revocation. An agency may be temporarily continued under the conditions specified in section 15-14-607.

(3) All acts of the agent that are within the scope of the agency and are committed during any period of disability, incapacity, or incompetency of the principal have the same effect and inure to the benefit of and bind the principal and his or her successors in interest as if the principal were competent and not disabled.

(4) Any agent acting on behalf of a principal under an agency instrument has the right to resign under the terms and conditions stated in the agency instrument. If the agency instrument does not specify the terms and conditions of resignation, an agent may resign by notifying the principal, or the principal's guardian or conservator if one has been appointed, in writing of the agent's resignation. The agent shall also notify in writing the successor agent, if any, and all reasonably ascertainable third parties who are affected by the resignation. In all cases, any party who receives notice of the resignation of an agent is bound by such notice.

15-14-605. Dissolution of marriage.

If an agency instrument appoints the principal's spouse as agent and a court enters a decree of dissolution of marriage or legal separation between the principal and spouse after the agency instrument is signed, the spouse shall be deemed to have died at the time of the decree for purposes of the agency.

15-14-606. Duty - standard of care - record-keeping - exoneration.

Unless otherwise agreed by the principal and agent in the agency instrument, an agent is under no duty to exercise the powers granted by the agency or to assume control of or responsibility for any of the principal's property, care, or affairs, regardless of the principal's physical or mental condition. Whenever the agent exercises the powers granted by the agency, the agent shall use due care to act in the best interests of the principal in accordance with the terms of the agency. Any agent who acts under an agency instrument shall be liable for any breach of legal duty owed by the agent to the principal under Colorado law. The agent shall keep a record of all receipts, disbursements, and significant actions taken under the agency. The agent shall not be liable for any loss due to the act or default of any other person. When exercising any powers under an agency during any period of disability of the principal, the agent shall be held to the standard of care of a fiduciary as specified in sections 15-16-302 and 15-14-418.

15-14-609. Agency - court relationship.

(1) Upon petition by any interested person, including the agent, after such notice to interested persons as the court directs and upon a finding by the court that the principal lacks the capacity to control or revoke the agency instrument:

(a) If the court finds that the agent is not acting for the benefit of the principal in accordance with the terms of the agency instrument or that the agent's action or inaction has caused or threatens substantial harm to the principal's person or property in a manner not authorized or intended by the principal, the court may order a guardian of the principal's person or a conservator of the principal's estate, or both, to exercise any powers of the principal under the agency instrument, including the power to revoke the agency, or may enter such other orders without appointment of a guardian or conservator as the court deems necessary to provide for the best interests of the principal; or

(b) If the court finds that the agency instrument requires interpretation, the court may construe the agency instrument and instruct the agent to act in accordance with its construction; except that the court may not amend the agency instrument. A court may order a guardian or conservator, or both, to exercise powers of the principal under the agency instrument.

(2) Proceedings under this section shall be commenced in the court where the guardian or conservator was appointed. If no Colorado guardian or conservator has been appointed, proceedings shall be commenced in the county where the principal resides. If the principal does not reside in Colorado, proceedings may be commenced in any county in the state.

(3) (a) If a guardian or conservator is appointed for the principal, the agent shall consult with the guardian or conservator during the continuance of the appointment on matters concerning the principal's financial affairs.

(b) A conservator has the same power to revoke, suspend, or terminate all or any part of the power of attorney or agency instrument as it relates to financial matters as the principal would have had if the principal were not disabled or incompetent.

(c) Subject to any limitation or restriction included in the letters of guardianship, a guardian has the same power to revoke, suspend, or terminate all or any part of the power of attorney or agency instrument as it relates to matters concerning the principal's personal care that the principal would have had if the principal were not disabled or incompetent, except with respect to medical treatment decisions made by an agent pursuant to sections 15-14-506 to 15-14-509. The exception included in this paragraph (c) shall not preclude a court from removing an agent in the event the agent becomes incapacitated or is unwilling or unable to serve as an agent.

15-16-302. Trustee's standard of care and performance.

Except as otherwise provided by the terms of the trust, the trustee shall observe the standards in dealing with the trust assets that would be observed by a prudent man dealing with the property of another, and if the trustee has special skills or is named trustee on the basis of representations of special skills or expertise, he is under a duty to use those skills.

Abuse of Representative Payee Authority

The Social Security Administration (SSA) specifies the procedures to follow in addressing suspected abuse of authority. It is important to note that a representative payee is appointed to manage Social Security funds *only*. A representative payee has no legal authority to manage non-Social Security income or medical matters.

The two types of representative payees are:

- An individual, such as a relative, friend, or other interested party.
- An organization or agency, such as a county department of social services or a private organization also referred to as a fee-for-service representative payee.

Individual representative payees are periodically asked by the SSA to complete a form that accounts for the funds received by the beneficiary. Rep payees are required by law to use the benefits properly. Misuse of benefits will require the rep payee to repay the misused funds to the beneficiary. If convicted of misuse of a beneficiary's benefits, the rep payee may be fined and/or imprisoned. The rep payee must also inform SSA about changes that may affect the beneficiary's eligibility for benefits.

The SSA visits **organizational representative payee** sites periodically to provide ongoing education for the organization about the organization's duties and responsibilities as a representative payee and improve lines of communication between the organization and SSA. These site visits include:

1) Six-Month Site Visit: Fee-for-service representative payees will be visited six months after an appointment.

2) Annual Certification: Fee-for-service representative payees are required to show each year that they continue to meet the requirements for charging a fee for service.

3) Site Reviews: Fee-for-service representative payees and certain other large organizational representative payees will be visited at least once every three years.

4) Random Reviews: Interim reviews of a random sample of organizational representative payees are conducted by the SSA.

Procedure to Address Abuse of Representative Payee Authority

1) Immediately **notify the SSA** Office of the Inspector General Hotline if you believe the rep payee has misused the benefits being issued to the beneficiary. Contact information includes:

   a. Hotline: 1-800-269-0271 (10:00 a.m. to 4:00 p.m. EST)
   b. Fax: (410) 597-0118
   c. Address: SSA Fraud Hotline, P.O. Box 17768, Baltimore, MD 21235

2) Provide as much **identifying information** as possible regarding the suspect, including:

   a. Name of the rep payee and the beneficiary, if known
   b. Social Security Number of the rep payee and the beneficiary, if known
   c. Date of birth of the rep payee and the beneficiary
   d. Details regarding the allegation, such as when and where the abuse took place, and how the abuse was committed

3) **SSA will investigate** the matter and a letter will be sent to the beneficiary stating whether misuse has or has not occurred.

4) If misuse has occurred, **SSA will determine if SSA was negligent** in appointing or monitoring the rep payee and inform the beneficiary in writing of SSA's conclusion.

5) **If SSA was negligent, SSA must pay whatever benefits were lost** through the misuse of benefits by the rep payee.

6) **If SSA was not negligent, an appeal may be filed.**

Resource

This section contains information on accessing statutes on the Internet, guidelines for guardians and conservators, and sample forms used in guardianship, conservatorship, and advance medical directives. *Please note: Forms shown in this section are meant to give a basic idea of the information required and are not meant to be used for official or legal purposes.*

Fundamental Principles for Guardians and Conservators of Adults

Principle 1

Guardians and conservators shall actively seek out alternatives to guardianship and conservatorship where appropriate.

Principle 2

Guardians and conservators shall actively work toward the goal of limiting or terminating the guardianship or conservatorship. To this end, guardians and conservators must encourage the ward or protected person in the appropriate restoration, maintenance, or development of maximum self-reliance and independence.

Principle 3

When wards and protected persons wishes and values are known guardians and conservators shall make decisions based on the principle of substituted judgment. When the person's own wishes and values are not known, guardians and conservators should actively pursue the best interests of the ward or protected person even though these interests may conflict with the interests of the community, neighbors, caretakers, families, and other third parties. In pursuing the best interests of the ward or protected person, the guardian or conservator must attempt to determine the desires and objectives of the person with respect to all matters, unless such desires or objectives are clearly not in the best interests of the ward or protected person.

Principle 4

Where a guardian has such authority, and a conservator has financial control, guardians and conservators shall maintain the ward or, if necessary, move the ward to the most normalized, and least restrictive, appropriate environment that manifests opportunity for independence and autonomy.

Principle 5

Guardians and conservators shall not exceed the bounds of their authority as described by the court and the laws and regulations under which they are appointed.

Principle 6

All wards and protected persons shall be accorded equal procedural protections and safeguards.

Principle 7

Guardians and conservators shall treat the ward or protected person with dignity and respect.

Principle 8

Guardians and conservators shall keep the affairs of the ward or protected person confidential, except: (1) for purposes of reporting to the court or the agency responsible for funding services; (2) when it is necessary to disclose such information for the best interests of the ward or protected person; or (3) when the ward or protected person, if capable, has given his/her informed consent to the disclosure of such information.

Adapted from Model Standards developed by the Center for Social Gerontology, Ann Arbor, Michigan in 1989 and published by the Subcommittee on Housing and Consumer Interest of the Select Committee on Aging, U.S. House of Representatives, One Hundred First Congress, in October 1989. The model principles were intended to apply to guardians and representative payees. They may also apply to conservators, as appropriate.

Accessing Statutes on the Internet

Statutes can be found on the Internet from the LexisNexis website through the following URL:

http://198.187.128.12/colorado/lpext.dll?f=templates&fn=fs-main.htm&2.0

OR through the State of Colorado home page located at www.colorado.gov

- Choose the "Government" link
- Choose "Colorado Revised Statutes." You will be directed to the LexisNexis Statute Manager website where a search can be done for all of Colorado's state statutes.

Basic Forms for Guardianship and Conservatorship

Directly following this page, you will find examples of the following forms used for Guardianship and Conservatorship proceedings.

- Instructions for Appointment of a Guardian
- Petition for Appointment of Guardian
- Guardian's Report
- Petition for Appointment of Conservator
- Petition for Termination of Conservatorship

Please Note: These forms are to be used as a guide *only*, not to file actual court documents. Please get actual court documents from the county courthouse or from the Internet website for the Colorado Judicial Branch, as explained below.

A complete list of forms may be found on and printed from the Internet. To access these forms, go directly to the probate forms page of the Judiciary website by using the following URL:

http://www.courts.state.co.us/chs/court/forms/selfhelpcenter.htm

OR start at the State of Colorado home page, located at www.colorado.gov and follow the links:

- Choose the "Government" link
- Scroll down to the Colorado State Judicial Branch heading and click on "Colorado State courts Home Page"
- On the Colorado Judicial Branch website choose the "Self Help Center" link
- On the next page choose "probate." All court forms related to guardianship and conservatorship are listed

INSTRUCTIONS FOR

APPOINTMENT OF A GUARDIAN (ADULT)

THESE STANDARD INSTRUCTIONS ARE FOR INFORMATIONAL PURPOSES ONLY AND DO NOT CONSTITUTE LEGAL ADVICE ABOUT YOUR CASE. IF YOU CHOOSE TO REPRESENT YOURSELF, YOU ARE BOUND BY THE SAME RULES AND PROCEDURES AS AN ATTORNEY.

If reviewing the instructions online, please view the relevant rules at **§15-14-301, et.seq.**
By accessing the Colorado Rules of Civil Procedure, you will be leaving the Colorado Judicial Branch's website at **www.courts.state.co.us**

GENERAL INFORMATION BEFORE YOU FILE YOUR CASE IN DISTRICT COURT

- ❏ The Respondent must be a resident in the county in which you are filing the petition, §15-14-108, C.R.S.
- ❏ A person interested in the welfare of the Respondent may file the case.

COMMON TERMS

- ☒ Petitioner: A person who files a Petition for the Appointment of a Guardian.
- ☒ Guardian: A person at least 21, resident or non-resident, who has qualified as a Guardian of a minor or incapacitated person based on an appointment by a parent(s) or by the court. Terms of the guardianship may be limited, emergency, and temporary.
- ☒ Interested Persons: The class of persons identified by Colorado Law who must be given notice of a guardianship proceeding.
- ☒ Letters: A formal notice identifying the authority of the Guardian.
- ☒ Incapacitated Person: An adult person who lacks sufficient understanding or capacity to make or communicate responsible decisions concerning that person's physical health, safety or self-care.
- ☒ Guardian Nominee: A person named in the petition to serve as the Guardian.
- ☒ Respondent: A person for whom the appointment of a guardian is required.
- ☒ Ward: A person for whom a Guardian has been appointed.

IF YOU DO NOT UNDERSTAND THIS INFORMATION, PLEASE CONTACT AN ATTORNEY.

FEES

The filing fee is $136.00. If you are unable to pay, you may qualify to file your case without the filing fee. To apply for this, complete the Motion to File Without Payment and Supporting Financial Affidavit (JDF 205) (see forms below) and submit the motion to the court.

Other fees that a party to the case may encounter are as follows:

- ❏ Certification of Orders $10.00

- ❏ Service Fees   Varies

135

❑ Copy of Documents   .75 per page

❑ The Court must appoint a court Visitor to investigate and report back to the court, for the purpose of determining if the Guardianship is in the best interest of the Respondent. The Respondent may be required to pay the hourly fee of the Court Visitor. Hourly rates vary between $20.00 to $200.00.

FORMS (To access the forms on the judicial website at **www.courts.state.co.us**, click either PDF or WORD by the title of the form.) You may complete the forms online or you may print them and type or print legibly in black ink.

❑	CPC 32	Petition for Appointment of Guardian	PDF	WORD
❑	CPC 18	Acceptance of Appointment	PDF	WORD
❑	CPC 18A	Irrevocable Power of Attorney	PDF	WORD
❑	CPC 33	Order Appointing Guardian	PDF	WORD
❑	CPC 2IP	Notice of Hearing to Interested Persons	PDF	WORD
❑	CPC 2R	Notice of Hearing to Respondent	PDF	WORD
❑	CPC 6	Notice of Hearing by Publication	PDF	WORD
❑	CPC 7P	Personal Service Affidavit	PDF	WORD
❑	CPC 8	Waiver of Notice	PDF	WORD
❑	CPC 17	Letters	PDF	WORD
❑	JDF 208	Application for court Appointed Counsel or Guardian ad Litem	PDF	WORD
❑	JDF 205	Motion to File Without Payment, Supporting Financial Affidavit	PDF	WORD
❑	CPC 2A	Notice of Appointment	PDF	WORD
❑	CPC 32GR	Guardian's Report	PDF	WORD

STEPS TO FILING YOUR CASE

❑ **Step 1: Complete the appropriate forms and check with your local district for additional filing requirements.**

    ❑ Petition for Appointment of Guardian (CPC 32). The Petitioner must complete all applicable sections on the form.

❑ Acceptance of Appointment (CPC 18). Place a check in the Guardian box on the form and have the nominated guardian sign the form and complete the address portion below the signature line.

❑ Irrevocable Power of Attorney (CPC 18A). This form must be completed **ONLY** if the proposed guardian lives out of state or plans to move out of state soon after the guardianship is granted. The nominated guardian must complete this form and have it signed before a notary public.

❑ Order Appointing Guardian (CPC 33). Complete caption only on the form. The Judge or Magistrate will complete the appropriate portions on the forms and sign the order at the time of the hearing, if your Petition is approved.

❑ Letters (CPC 17). Complete caption only on the form. The Court will complete the appropriate portions on the forms and sign the form following the appointment of the guardian.

❑ Notice of Hearing by Publication (CPC 6). If at the time of filing, you do not know the whereabouts of the interested persons to notify them of the Petition filed and the hearing date, you may submit the Notice to the Court with a self-addressed stamped envelope to the court to be returned to the Petitioner. Complete as many notices as necessary.

❑ **Step 2:** You are ready to file your case with the court. Provide the Court with the documents completed as described in Step 1 above, and pay the filing fee of $136.00.

❑ You may receive a hearing date from the clerk at the time of filing. The date and time of this hearing is important, as you will need to complete the appropriate Notice to the Respondent and Notice to the Interested Person per Step 3 and 4. You must serve the interested persons listed on the Petition, unless the Waiver of Notice (CPC 8) was completed. Any interested person may waive notice by completing this form.

❑ The Court shall appoint a visitor who shall interview the Respondent in person, per §15-14-305(3)(4)(5), C.R.S. The duties and reporting requirements of the visitor are limited to the relief requested in the petition.

❑ **Step 3:** Determine the method of service (Personal Service or Service by Publication) based on your knowledge of the whereabouts of the Respondent and complete the appropriate forms.

❑ **Personal Service:**

❑ Notice of Hearing to Respondent (CPC 2R) and Personal Service Affidavit (CPC 7P). You must personally serve the Respondent at least ten days before the hearing. (Failure to properly serve the Respondent voids the proceeding and the hearing cannot be held). Helpful Hints to complete personal service:

❑ Take a copy of the Notice of Hearing to Respondent (CPC 2R) and Personal Service Affidavit (CPC 7P) and copies of all documents filed with the Court to the sheriff, a private process server, or anyone over the age of eighteen NOT involved in the case for service.

❑ Be sure to direct the sheriff, private process server, or person serving the documents to return the Personal Service Affidavit (CPC 7P) to you.

❑ You should then file the Personal Service Affidavit (CPC 7P) together with the original Notice of Hearing to Respondent (CPC 2 R) with the Clerk of the Court.

❑ **Service by Publication:**

❑ Notice of Hearing by Publication (CPC 6). If you **DO NOT** have the correct address for the Respondent, complete the Notice and submit to the court with a self-addressed stamped envelope to be returned to you.

❑ Once you receive the signed documents, you must have the Notice (CPC 6) published in a newspaper of general circulation in the county where the case was filed. The notice shall be published once a week for three consecutive weeks, in a newspaper of general circulation in the county where the hearing is to be held with the last date of the publication to be at least ten days before the date of the hearing.

❑ You must request an affidavit from the newspaper after publication is completed. This affidavit of publication, prepared by the newspaper, will serve as proof that the Notice (CPC 6) was published.

❑ When filing the proof of publication, the party giving notice shall also file an affidavit, verified by oath, stating the facts that warranted the use of publication for service of the Notice and stating the efforts, if any, that have been made to obtain personal service by mail. The affidavit shall also state the address, or last known address, of each person served by publication or state that the person's address or identity is unknown.

❑ **Step 4:**   Notice of Hearing to Interested Persons (CPC 2IP). If you have the correct address as identified on the Petition for the interested persons, complete all portions. You may need several forms, depending on the number of interested persons you plan to notify of the proposed guardianship. Mail copies of all documents filed with the court and the completed Notice of Hearing to Interested Persons (CPC 2IP) at least ten days before the hearing. Check the list below to determine interested persons that are applicable to your circumstances. Complete the Certificate of Service on the second page of CPC 2IP, listing the names and addresses of all interested persons and file with the Court on or before your hearing.
  1. The spouse of the incapacitated person, if married.
  2. The parents of the incapacitated person, if any.
  3. The adult children of the incapacitated person, if any.
  4. Any Guardian or Conservator currently acting for the incapacitated person.
  5. Any person who has care and custody of the incapacitated person, including the Respondent's treating physician.
  6. Any adult with whom the Respondent has resided for more than six months within one year before the filing of the Petition, §15-14-304(2)(b)(I)(A)
  7. Any adult relative nearest of kin, if there is no spouse, parent, or adult children.
  8. Any legal representative of the Respondent
  9. Any nominated person as guardian by the Respondent.

❑ **Step 5:**   Hearing

❑ The Petitioner and Respondent must appear at the hearing, unless excused by the Court.
❑ The Respondent may participate in the Hearing to present evidence regarding his or her incapacitation.
❑ Be prepared to present evidence that the interested persons are aware of the proceedings and that they consent to the Guardianship.

❑ **Step 6:**   Requirements after the Court appoints a Guardian.
❑ Complete a Guardian Report (CPC 32GR). This report must be submitted to the Court within 60 days following the appointment. This report must also be provided to the persons listed in the Order.
❑ A "Notice of Appointment" (CPC 2-A) must be mailed to all parties with a copy of the Court order within 30 days and the original filed with the Court.
❑ Check with the Court to determine if the Petitioner is required to submit an annual Guardian Report (CPC 32GR). The purpose of the report is to report to the Court and interested persons the well being of the Ward.

The responsibilities of the guardian terminate upon the death of the Ward or upon order of the Court. The Court may terminate the Guardianship if the Ward no longer meets the standard for establishing the Guardianship.

❑ District Court ❑ Denver Probate Court
_____ County, Colorado
Court Address:

_____
_____

IN THE MATTER OF:

Respondent

▲   ▲

COURT USE ONLY

Attorney or Party Without Attorney (Name and Address):

Phone Number: E-mail:
FAX Number: Atty. Reg.#.:

Case Number:

Division   Courtroom

PETITION FOR APPOINTMENT OF GUARDIAN

1. Petitioner, _____
   _____ (name)
   _____ (residence and current address if different)
   _____ (Relationship to respondent)

   ❑   is interested in the welfare of the respondent. (State nature of interest.)

   ❑   is the above respondent.

2. The respondent, age _____, was born on (date) _____ and resides at _____
   _____, in the County of _____, State of Colorado.

   ❑   Under this guardianship, the respondent's dwelling is likely to be changed to
   _____. The reason for the change

   of dwelling is _____.

3. Venue for this proceeding is proper in this county because the respondent

   ❑   resides in this county.
   ❑   is present in this county. *Emergency or temporary substitute guardianships only.* (§15-14-108(2), C.R.S.)
   ❑   is admitted to an institution pursuant to an order of a court of competent jurisdiction sitting in this county.

4. An appointment of a guardian for the respondent has been made. *See attached statement.*

5. The respondent is unable to effectively receive or evaluate information or both or make or communicate decisions to such an extent that the individual lacks the ability to satisfy essential requirements for physical health, safety, or self-care, even with appropriate and reasonably available technological assistance. (§15-14-102(5), C.R.S.)

139

6. Guardianship is necessary because: (State the nature and extent of the respondent's alleged lack of capacity. §15-14-304(2)(g). C.R.S.) _____

_____

_____

_____

_____

Attach physician's letter or professional evaluation by qualified person. (§15-14-306, C.R.S.)

7. The following is a general statement of the respondent's property, together with an estimate of its value, including any insurance or pension, and the source and amount of any other anticipated income or receipts: (§15-14-304(2)(i), C.R.S.)

Description and Location   **Estimated Value or Income**

8. ❑   Limited guardianship is requested. The following powers should be granted to the limited guardian: (§15-14-304(2)(h), C.R.S.) _____

_____

_____

❑   Unlimited guardianship is requested. The reason why limited guardianship is inappropriate is: (§15-14-304(2)(h), C.R.S.) _____

_____

_____

The respondent's identified needs cannot be met by less restrictive means, including use of appropriate and reasonably available technological assistance. (§15-14-311(1)(a)(II), C.R.S.)

9. ❑   It is necessary to appoint an emergency guardian for the respondent because of the likelihood of substantial harm to the respondent's health, safety, or welfare, an emergency exists and no other person appears to have authority and willingness to act in the circumstances. (§15-14-312(1), C.R.S.) The nature of the emergency is: _____

_____

_____

10. Petitioner nominates _____

(name, address and telephone number of petitioner's nominee for guardian)

_____

who has priority for appointment as guardian because: (§15-14-310, C.R.S.) _____

_____

_____

_____

140

_____

_____

_____

11. The name and address of the respondent's spouse, or if none, an adult with whom the respondent has resided for more than six (6) months within one (1) year before filing this petition is: _____

_____

_____

_____

The name and address of each of respondent's adult children is: _____

_____

_____

The names and addresses of respondent's parents are: _____

_____

If the respondent has neither spouse, adult child, nor parent, give the name and address of at least one of the adults nearest in kinship to the respondent who can be found with reasonable efforts: _____

_____

_____

The name and address of each person responsible for care or custody of the respondent, including the respondent's treating physician: _____

_____

_____

The name and address of each legal representative of the respondent is: (§15-14-102(6), C.R.S.) _____

_____

The name and address of each person nominated as guardian by the respondent is: (§15-14-310, C.R.S.)

_____

_____

If respondent's nomination is by written instrument, attach a copy.

The persons listed above will be given notice of the time and place for hearing on this petition. (§§15-14-304(2)(a)-(f), 15-14-309(1)(2), C.R.S.)

PETITIONER REQUESTS that the Court set a time and place of hearing; that the Court appoint a visitor; that after notice and hearing the court find that the above person is incapacitated; that the Court appoint the nominee as guardian; and that Letters of Guardianship be issued;

❏ that the Court appoint an emergency guardian and appoint counsel to represent the respondent throughout the emergency guardianship. (§15-14-305(1), C.R.S.)
❏ Petitioner further requests _____

Date: _____

_____   _____
Signature of Attorney for Petitioner   Signature of Petitioner

☐ District Court   ☐ Denver Probate Court
_____
County, Colorado
Court Address:

_____

IN THE MATTER OF:

Ward

Attorney or Party Without Attorney (Name and Address):	Case Number:
Phone Number: E-mail:	
FAX Number: Atty. Reg. #:	Division Courtroom

COURT USE ONLY

GUARDIAN'S REPORT

GUARDIAN'S INFORMATION:

Guardian's Name _____

Home Address: _____

_____

Including P.O. Box _____

_____

& Phone Number

(____)_____

_____

Work Address:

_____

Including P.O. Box   _____

_____

& Phone Number   _____

(_____)_____

_____

WARD'S INFORMATION:

Ward's Name _____

Current Address: _____

_____

Include Name of Living   _____

_____

Center or Nursing Home

_____

& Phone Number   _____

(_____)_____

_____

This format is intended as a guide to guardians and their lawyers. The elements of a care plan are highly variable, and the direction of a care plan is dynamic, since the needs of your ward may change significantly over time. Nevertheless, focusing on answers to these guiding questions will assist the parties and the Court. The initial guardian's report should be filed within sixty (60) days after the guardian is appointed. Thereafter, the guardian's report should be filed annually unless otherwise ordered.

⇒

⇒ I.   **Basic condition of the ward**

A. What is your ward's physical and medical condition?

_____

_____

_____

_____

B. Describe the nature and extent of your ward's mental incapacity.

_____

_____

_____

_____

C. What are the current prescribed medications? What is each medication for?

_____

_____

_____

_____

D. Have there been any recent hospitalizations or trips to the emergency room? If so, please describe for
    what and the dates of each event.

_____

_____

_____

_____

E. What is the name, address and telephone number of the ward's treating physician?

_____

_____

_____

F. What is the name, address and telephone number of the professional who did the last assessment of
    mental incapacity?

_____

_____

_____

G. Is there need for further assessment?

_____

_____

_____

_____

H. Is there need for other professional evaluations? If so, describe.

_____

_____

_____

_____

II. Medical Decision-Making

A. Who has authority to make medical decisions on behalf of your ward?

_____

_____

B. What is your ward's "COR" or "code" status?
(For example, Full COR, No COR or Do Not Resuscitate.)

_____

_____

_____

_____

C. What are your ward's current advance medical directives, if any? Describe any health care power of attorney, living will, cardiopulmonary ("CPR") directives, or other advance medical directives, and attach copies.

_____

_____

_____

_____

D. If your ward has not made such directives, what do you believe would be the best approach to these issues?

_____

_____

_____

III. Placement and Care Supervision

A. Where is your ward residing now and what kind of facility is it? (For example, is it a private residence, assisted living, or nursing home, etc.?)

_____

_____

_____

_____

B. Do you anticipate needing to change your ward's residence? If so, when and why?

_____

_____

_____

_____

C. What services are currently provided to your ward? Include medical, educational, vocational, rehabilitative therapies, and other services.

_____

_____

_____

_____

_____

D. Who supervises your ward's care and treatment on a daily basis? _____

E. How often do you communicate with this care supervisor? _____

F. How often do you visit your ward, and how long are your visits? _____

_____

_____

G. When was the last time you saw the ward in person? Where did this visit take place? How long was the visit? _____

⇒ _____

H. What arrangements have been made for your ward to be involved in social events, spiritual activities, or other community programs? Do you take the ward or is transportation provided?

_____

_____

IV. Financial Matters

A. What is the source of payment for medical services and for room and board?

_____

_____

_____

B. Who is the designated Representative Payee for Social Security and other income benefits?

_____

_____

_____

C. Are all payments up-to-date for medical services and for room and board? _____

_____

D. Are there sufficient financial resources to take care of your ward? If not, what do you believe is the best way to handle this problem?

_____

_____

_____

_____

E. Do you have possession or control of the ward's assets or income? ❑ No.   ❑ Yes. If yes, you must also file an inventory of assets on CPC Form 20. An annual accounting on CPC Form 43 will be required along with the Guardian's Annual Report.

_____

_____

_____

_____

V. Other Issues

A. What specific problems do you experience or foresee, either for yourself as guardian or for your ward? How do you believe it will be best to handle each problem?

_____

_____

_____

_____

_____

_____

B. Do you as guardian have any other concerns or comments?

_____

_____

_____

_____

_____

C. Do you believe the ward's care is adequate and appropriate?

_____

_____

_____

_____

_____

D. Summarize your activities as guardian on behalf of your ward.

_____

_____

_____

_____

_____

E. How does your ward participate in decision-making?

_____

_____

_____

_____

_____

_____

F. Do you believe the current plan for care, treatment or rehabilitation is in the ward's best interest? If your answer is no, describe what changes would be appropriate.

_____
_____
_____
_____
_____
_____
_____
_____

G. What are your plans for care during the next year?

_____
_____
_____
_____
_____
_____

H. Do you recommend that the guardianship continue?

_____
_____
_____
_____
_____

I. What changes would you make to the guardianship?

_____
_____
_____
_____
_____
_____
_____
_____
_____
_____

⇒

Dated: _____   _____
                                        Signature of Guardian

149

❑ District Court ❑ Denver Probate Court
_____ County, Colorado
Court Address:

_____

IN THE MATTER OF THE ESTATE OF:

Respondent

▲ **COURT USE ONLY** ▲

Attorney or Party Without Attorney (Name and Address):	Case Number:
Phone Number: E-mail: FAX Number: Atty. Reg.#:	Division Courtroom

PETITION FOR APPOINTMENT OF CONSERVATOR FOR ❑ Minor ❑ Adult

1. Petitioner, _____
                                                  (name)

   _____
                  (residence and current address if different)

   _____
                  (relationship to respondent)

   ❑   is interested in the estate, financial affairs or welfare of the protected person. (State nature of interest.)

   _____.

   ❑   is the above person.
   ❑   is a person who would be adversely affected by lack of effective management of the respondent's property
       and business.

2. The respondent, age _____, was born on (date) _____ and resides at _____

   _____ in the County of _____, State of Colorado.

   ❑   Under this conservatorship, the respondent's dwelling is likely to be changed to

   _____. The reason for the change

   of dwelling is _____.

3. Venue for this proceeding is proper in this county because the respondent

   ❑ resides in this county.

150

❑ does not reside in Colorado, but property of the person is located in this county.

4. The name and address of the person's guardian, if any, is

_____

_____

_____.

5. A conservatorship or other protective order is in the best interest of the respondent because: (§15-14-403(2)(h), C.R.S.)

_____

_____

6. ❑   A conservator is required because the respondent is a minor and: (§15-14-401(1)(a), C.R.S.)
   - ❑   the minor owns money or property that requires management or protection which cannot otherwise be provided; or
   - ❑   the minor has or may have business affairs which may be put at risk or prevented because his or her age; or
   - ❑   the minor requires money for support and education, and protection is necessary or desirable to obtain or provide money.

7. ❑   A conservator is required because the respondent (whether an adult or minor) is unable to manage property and business affairs because of an inability to effectively receive or evaluate information or both or to make or communicate decisions, even with the use of appropriate and reasonably available technological assistance, or because the respondent is missing, detained, or unable to return to the United States, and: (§15-14-401(1)(b)(I), C.R.S.)
   - ❑   the respondent has property which will be wasted or dissipated unless proper management is provided; or
   - ❑   the respondent, or persons entitled to the respondent's support, require money for support, care, education, health, and welfare, and protection is necessary or desirable to obtain or provide money.
   - ❑   The nature and extent of the respondent's disability or impairment is: (§15-14-403(2)(b), C.R.S.) _____

_____

   - ❑   The time and nature of respondent's disappearance or detention and any efforts to locate respondent are: (§15-14-403(2)(c), C.R.S.) _____

_____

8.   The following is a general statement of the property of the person, together with an estimate of the value, including any insurance or pension, and the source and amount of any other anticipated income or receipts: (§15-14-403(2)(g), C.R.S.)

Description and Location	Estimated Value or Income

9. ❑   Limited conservatorship is requested. The following powers should be granted to the limited conservator: (§15-14-403(3)(c), C.R.S.) _____

151

❏ Unlimited conservatorship is requested. The reason why limited conservatorship is inappropriate is: §15-14-403(3)(c), C.R.S. _____

10. ❏ It is necessary to appoint a special conservator for the respondent until a hearing can be held on the petition because: (§§15-14-405(2), (15-14-406(7), C.R.S.) _____

❏ It is necessary to appoint a special conservator to assist in the accomplishment of a protective arrangement or other authorized transaction. (§15-14-412(3), C.R.S.) _____

11. Petitioner nominates _____
(name, address and telephone number of petitioner's nominee for conservator)

who has priority for appointment as conservator because: (§15-14-413, C.R.S.) _____

⇒ The name and address of the respondent's spouse, or if none, an adult with whom the respondent has resided for more than six (6) months within one year before filing this petition is: _____

The name and address of each of respondent's adult children is: _____

The names and addresses of respondent's parents are: _____

If the respondent has neither spouse, adult child nor parent, give the name and address of at least one (1) of the adults nearest in kinship to the respondent who can be found with reasonable efforts: _____

The name and address of each person responsible for care or custody of the respondent, including the respondent's treating physician: _____

The name and address of each legal representative of the respondent is: (§15-14-102(6), C.R.S.) _____

The name and address of each person nominated as conservator by the respondent is: (§15-14-403(4)(b), C.R.S.) _____

If respondent's nomination is by written instrument, attach a copy.

The persons listed above will be given notice of the time and place for hearing on this petition. (§§15-14-403(2)(a)-(f), 15-14-404(1)(2), C.R.S.)

PETITIONER REQUESTS that the Court set a time and place of hearing; that the Court appoint a visitor; that after notice and hearing the Court find that appointment of a conservator is proper; that the Court determine those persons to whom notice of hearing should be given on any subsequent petition or motion for an order; that the Court appoint the nominee as conservator and that Letters of Conservatorship be issued;

    ☐   that the court appoint a special conservator. (§§15-14-406(7) or 15-14-412(3), C.R.S.)

    ☐   Petitioner further requests _____.

Date: _____

_____
Signature of Attorney for Petitioner

_____
Signature of Petitioner

153

☐ District Court ☐ Denver Probate Court _____ County, Colorado Court Address: **IN THE MATTER OF THE ESTATE OF:** **Protected Person**	▲ ▲ ***COURT USE ONLY***
Attorney or Party Without Attorney (Name and Address):	Case Number:
Phone Number: E-mail: FAX Number: Atty. Reg. #:	Division Courtroom

PETITION FOR TERMINATION OF CONSERVATORSHIP

1. *Petitioner (name)* _____, *resides at (include current address if different)*

    _____
    _____.

    ☐   is the conservator of the estate and affairs of the protected person.

    ☐   is the protected person.

    ☐   is a person interested in the protected person's welfare (State nature of interest.)

    _____

    _____

    _____

2. Petitioner requests that this conservatorship be terminated for the following reason(s):

    ☐   The conservatorship was created solely due to the minority of the protected person. The protected person was born on (date) _____, and has attained the age of twenty-one (21) years. (§15-14-430, C.R.S.)

    ☐   The protected person's disability or impairment has ended. Describe:

    _____

154

_____

❑ The protected person died on or about (date) _____ .

❑ There are insufficient assets of the estate to warrant continued administration. Remarks:

_____

_____

_____

_____

_____

❑ Other:

_____

_____

_____

_____

_____

_____

3. The following persons were designated to receive notice of subsequent actions in the Order appointing the conservator and are required by law to be given notice of the time and place of hearing on this Petition:

Name   Address   Relationship to Protected
Person

4. The Conservator has collected and managed the assets of this estate, filed the required inventory, financial plan, and conservator reports, paid all lawful claims against this estate, and performed all other acts required of a conservator by law.

Petitioner requests that the Court set a time and place of hearing; that notice be given to all interested persons as provided by law; that after notice and hearing, the Court determine that the reason for the conservatorship has ceased and enter an order directing the conservator to distribute all assets of the estate in the amount and manner set forth in the attached Schedule of Distribution, and that accountings be:

☐ accepted as filed.
☐ dispensed with.
☐ approved after audit.
☐ other:

_____

_____

_____

_____

_____

_____

_____

_____

_____

_____

_____.

Petitioner requests that the court approve payment of all fees, costs, and expenses of administration, as set forth in the Conservator's Final Report, as well as those previously paid.

Petitioner further requests that, upon filing final receipts, appropriate instruments evidencing transfer of title, or evidence confirming the ordered distribution pursuant to the Schedule of Distribution, the conservator and any surety on the conservator's bond be released and discharged from all liability arising in connection with the performance of conservator's duties, and that the administration of this conservatorship be terminated.

Date: _____

_____
Signature of Attorney for Petitioner   Signature of Petitioner

Basic Forms for Medical Durable Power of Attorney and Medical Advance Directives

Directly following this page, you will find examples of the following forms used for medical durable power of attorney and other types of medical advance directives.

- CPR Directive
- Living Will (Declaration as to Medical or Surgical Treatment)
- Medical Durable Power of Attorney
- Organ and/or Tissue Donation

Notice of Patient or Authorized Agent's Directive
to Withhold Cardiopulmonary Resuscitation (CPR)
State of Colorado

Patient's Name: _____

Name of : Authorized agent, proxy,
guardian/parent(s) of minor child (if applicable): _____

Date of Birth: ___/___/___ Gender: ☐ Male ☐ Female Eye Color: _____ Hair Color: _____

Race/Ethnicity: ☐ Asian or Pacific Islander   ☐ Black, non-Hispanic ☐ White, non-Hispanic
 ☐ American Indian of Alaska Native   ☐ Hispanic   ☐ Other

Name of hospice program (if applicable): _____

Attending Physician's Name: _____

Physician's Address: _____

Physician's telephone: (___) _____ Physician's License #: _____

Directive made on this date: _____, pursuant to Colorado Revised Statue 15-18.6-101.
 (Month, day, year)

Check only one of the following (as appropriate):

☐ Patient: I am over the age of 18 years, of sound mind and acting voluntarily. It is my desire to initiate this directive on my behalf, and **I have been advised that the expected result of executing this directive is my death in the event that my heart or breathing stops or malfunctions.**

☐ **Authorized agent/proxy/legally authorized guardian/parent(s) of minor child: I am over the age of 18 years, of** sound mind, and I am legally authorized to act on behalf of the patient named above in the issuance of this directive. **I have been advised that the expected result of executing this directive is the death of the patient, in the event the patient's heart or breathing stops or malfunctions.**

I hereby direct emergency medical services personnel, health care providers, and any other person to withhold cardiopulmonary resuscitation in **the event** that my/the patient's heart or breathing stops or malfunctions. I understand that this directive does not apply to other medical interventions for comfort care. If I/the patient am/is admitted to a health care facility, his directive shall be implemented as a physician's order, pending further physician's orders.

Use of original signatures on each page of this form makes each page an original document.

_____
Signature of ☐ Patient or ☐ Authorized agent/proxy/legally
 authorized guardian/parent(s) of minor child

_____
Signature of Attending Physician

Consent to the following tissue donation is optional. These tissue donations do not require resuscitation: **I hereby make an anatomical gift, to be effective upon my death of:** ☐ **Any needed tissues.** ☐ **The following tissues:**
☐ Skin ☐ Cornea ☐ Bone, related tissues and tendons. Donor/Agent Signature: _____

The CPR program is being administered by the Colorado Department of Public Health & Environment.
CPR directive forms administered by the CDPHE contain the blue "CPR" design in the background and the Colorado Directive logo.

Living Will

DECLARATION AS TO MEDICAL OR SURGICAL TREATMENT

I,_____ being of sound mind and at least eighteen years of age, direct
that my life shall
(Name of declarant)
not be artificially prolonged under the circumstances set forth below and hereby
declare that:

1) If at any time my attending physician and one other physician certify in
   writing that:
   a. I have an injury, disease or illness which is not curable or reversible and
      which, in their judgment, is a terminal condition; and
   b. For a period of seven consecutive *days* or more, I have been
      unconscious, comatose or *otherwise* incompetent so as to be unable to
      make or communicate responsible decisions concerning my person; then
      I direct that, in accordance with Colorado law, life-sustaining procedures
      shall be withdrawn and withheld pursuant to the terms of Ibis declaration;
      it being understood that life-sustaining procedures shall not include any
      medical procedure or intervention for nourishment considered necessary
      by the attending physician to provide comfort or alleviate pain. However, I
      may specifically direct, in accordance with Colorado *law* that artificial
      nourishment be withdrawn or withheld pursuant to the terms of *this*
      declaration.
2) In the event that the only procedure I am being provided is artificial
   nourishment, I direct that one of the following actions be taken:
   a. _____ (initials of declarant) Artificial nourishment shall not be continued
      when it is the only procedure being provided; or
   b. _____ (initials of declarant) Artificial nourishment shall be continued for
      _____ days when it is the only procedure being provided; or
   c. _____ (initials of declarant) Artificial nourishment shall be continued when it is
      the only procedure being provided.
3) I execute this declaration as my free and voluntary act this_____day of this
   month _____, in this year of _____.

                                                   By

                                                   _____
                                                   —
                                                   (Declarant)

The foregoing instrument was signed and declared by _____to be
his/her declaration, in the presence of us, who, in his/her presence, in the presence of
each other, and at his/her request, have signed our names below as witnesses, and we
declare that, at the time of the execution of this instrument, the declarant, according to
our best knowledge and belief, was of sound mind and under no constraint or undue

influence. We further declare that neither of *us* is: 1) a physician.; 2) the declarant's physician or an employee of his/her physician; 3) art employee or a patient *of the health care facility* in which the declarant is a patient; or 4) a beneficiary or creditor of the estate of the declarant.

Dated at _____ Colorado, this _____ day of _____, in the year _____.

_____   _____
(Signature of Witness)   (Signature of Witness)
Address: _____   Address: _____
_____   _____

OPTIONAL

STATE OF COLORADO, County of _____
Subscribed and sworn to or affirmed before me by _____, the declarant, and_____
witnesses, as the voluntary act and deed of the declarant, this _____ day of _____, in the year _____.
My commission expires:

_____
Notary Public

160

Medical Durable Power of Attorney for Health Care Decisions

1). I, _____, Declarant, hereby appoint:
   (Print or Type Your Name)

_____
Name of Agent

_____
Agent's Home Telephone Number

_____
Agent's Work Telephone Number

_____
Agent's Home Address

as my agent to make health care decisions for me if and when I am unable to make my own health care decisions. This gives my agent the power to consent, to refuse or stop any health care, treatment, service or diagnostic procedure, My agent also has the authority to talk with health care personnel, get information and sign forms necessary to carry out those decisions.
   If the person named as my agent is not available or is unable to act as my agent, then I appoint the following person(s) to serve in the order listed below:

2. _____   3. _____
      Agent Name   Agent Name

   _____   _____
      Home Telephone #   Home Telephone #

   _____   _____
      Work Telephone #   Work Telephone #

By this document I intend to create a **Medical Durable Power of Attorney** which shall take effect upon my incapacity to make my own health care decisions and shall continue during that incapacity.
   My agent shall make health care decisions as I may direct below or as I make known to him or her in some other way. If I have not expressed a choice about the health care in question, my agent shall base his/her decision on what he/she believes to be in my best interest.

   (A) Statement of desires concerning life-prolonging care, treatment, services, and
       procedures:

   _____
   _____
   _____
   _____
   _____

   (B) Special provisions and limitations:

   _____
   _____
   _____
   _____

BY SIGNING HERE, I INDICATE THAT I UNDERSTAND THE PURPOSE AND EFFECT OF THIS DOCUMENT.

_____
SIGNATURE OF PERSON CREATING MEDICAL DURABLE POWER OF ATTORNEY (DECLARANT)
DATE _____

(Optional But Recommended)
Colorado law does not require this instrument to be witnessed; however, it is recommended to obtain the signature of two witnesses or a notary. This is not required by Colorado law but may make this document more acceptable in other states.

WITNESS: WITNESS:
Signature: _____   Signature: _____
Home Address: _____   Home Address: _____

_____   _____
Date: _____   Date: _____

Organ and/or Tissue Donation

I hereby make an anatomical gift, to be effective upon my death, of:
    A.____ Any needed organs/tissues
    B.____ The following organs/tissues:

_____

Donor signature: _____

CPSIA information can be obtained
at www.ICGtesting.com
Printed in the USA
LVHW100311261019
635429LV00004BA/26/P

9 781298 052766